Editorial Direction
GHISLAINE BAVOILLOT

Artistic Direction
MARC WALTER

Typesetting
BELA VISTA

Photoengraving
ARCIEL Graphic

Translation from the French
BARBARA MELLOR

Adaptation and Editing
KATE SWAINSON

Printed by CANALE, TURIN

Original title: *Leçons de Fleurs*
Copyright © Flammarion 1997

For the English translation:
Copyright © Flammarion 1998

Flammarion
26 rue Racine
75006 Paris

ISBN: 2-08013-651-8

Numéro d'édition: FA 365101

Dépôt légal: March 1998

Printed in Italy

Library of Congress Cataloging-in-Pub

Philippe.
[Leçons de Fleurs. English]
Flower arranging in the French style / P
Landri ; photographs by Christophe Dugied ; te
Vleeschouwer.
p.   cm.
ISBN 2-08-013651-8 (hb)
I. Flower arrangement, French.   I. Landri, Pierre.
II. Vleeschouwer, Olivier de.   III. Title.
SB450.73.B713   1998
745.92'24'0944——dc21   98-11748

Pierre Brinon and Philippe Landri

Photographs by Christophe Dugied

Text by Olivier de Vleeschouwer

Flower Arranging

in the French Style

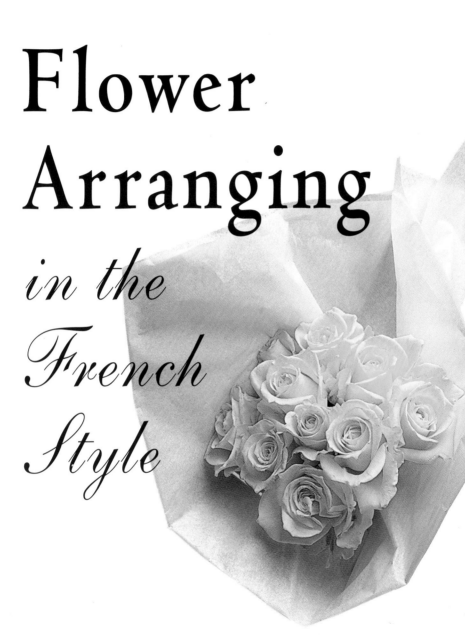

Flammarion

Paris – New York

Contents

The first posy

"We would say we were going out to pick three roses, two trails of clematis, and a sprig of alchemilla..." This is how a book should start, with a story you tell yourself and which, quite suddenly, you want to share with others. 🥀 But stories about flowers are only for adults

Mille Feuilles express their passion for profusion and contrasting textures in dense arrangements such as this posy, which combines softly opened crimson roses, small cherry-red chrysanthemums, and delicate wax flowers.

who have not quite cut themselves loose from the strings of their childhood, whose boots will always be just a little muddy, and who will always remember the forbidden pleasures of fruit stolen from the bottom of someone's garden. Nowadays everyone wants their own garden, for better or worse. Often this is a passing fancy which fades along with the first lost treasure or prematurely wilted rose, to be recollected with a wry smile. One thing is certain, however: fashions may come and go, but nothing will stop the peonies from flowering in May. Nature is lavish with such reassuringly dependable fixed points. 🥀 Who was it meant for, that first posy of your childhood with the stems all anyhow and different lengths? Did it last an hour, a day, or perhaps longer? What matters is that somewhere, in someone's memory, it is still fresh. Every bunch of daisies arranged with clumsy care in an old jam jar will have left its mark. Who was it for? A mother on her birthday, a cuddly grandmother, some other adored person? The details may fade, but one certainty remains: that first posy is always intended for someone special. 🥀 Giving a posy is giving pleasure, saying with flowers what you could never say in words, or not so well. It is a simple gesture, heavy with symbolism, and yet carried out with such perfect innocence. The child who is filled with wonder will swiftly learn that the quickest way to almost anyone's heart is via a posy of flowers, a precious revelation that is rapidly followed by the discovery that daisies are as exquisite as roses if gathered and arranged with love. We have to resign ourselves to

Each posy is carefully wrapped in a combination of toning tissue papers, making a gift that is as pleasurable to give as to receive.

the fact that nothing will ever again quite match the magic of that first simple nosegay of wild flowers. The skill lies in preserving the wonderment that went into the making of it. And if that child, when he grows up, should turn his love of flowers into a profession, let him always remember—however professional he may be—the simplicity of that first gesture. "We would say we were going out to pick three roses, two trails of clematis, and a sprig of alchemilla..." That is how a book should start, like an invitation to a voyage. And with the florists of Mille Feuilles as our guides, enchantment awaits round every corner. Here are ways of creating that magical element of surprise, from a sophisticated arrangement of dramatic, restrained elegance to an artless posy, fresh as a spring morning; from a voluptuous display of passionate reds and carmines to an unashamedly romantic pastel-tinted nosegay. And such surprise can be achieved by anybody, regardless of their skill in flower arranging. For if beauty is only the promise of happiness, as Stendhal claimed, following in the footsteps of Mille Feuilles is one certain way of keeping that promise.

When you open the door of the Mille Feuilles shop in the Marais district of Paris, you enter a world—part house, part garden—in which flowers in all their many colors and perfumes reign supreme. Quantities of vases, chandeliers, old furniture, and books, all engulfed in an avalanche of luxuriant floral displays, contribute to the cosy atmosphere.

Mille feuilles, mille fleurs

Anyone who has visited the Mille Feuilles shop in the Marais district of Paris will know that the owners' love of flowers is inseparable from their passion for interior decoration. For Pierre Brinon and Philippe Landri, *creating this unique space was the long-awaited fulfilment of a desire to bring flowers alive in warm, intimate surroundings in which their clients would immediately feel at ease. Conceived as a domestic interior waiting only to be decked with flowers, the shop mingles antique* objets, *household linen, china, and small pieces of furniture with quantities of vases, brimming with wonderful flowers.* Because a love of flowers is also a love of sharing that special magic with others, making a bouquet of flowers is always, ultimately, a gesture of love. This, in any case, is the way the crea-

tors of Mille Feuilles view their profession. Whether they are simply arranging armfuls of narcissi or concocting more elaborate compositions, their inventiveness and motivation never lose that inimitable dash of inspiration, and their touchstone remains constant: to delight the eye and cheer the heart. Although they have no hard-and-fast *"recipes," Pierre Brinon and Philippe Landri decided to celebrate the tenth anniversary of Mille Feuilles by sharing the secrets of their success, and of their distinctive combination of elegance and simplicity, with a wider public.* An adventurous approach to color *and form, combined with their unfailing emphasis on the close rapport between flowers and interior decoration, has earned them an enviable reputation not only among their regular clientele but also among celebrities from the Parisian film and fashion worlds. They are increasingly commissioned to style the venues for prestigious occasions, and you have*

Peonies, lilac, and sweet peas (right), viburnum, euphorbias, and anemones (below) are some of the garden flowers prized by Mille Feuilles for their flawed grace and dewy freshness.

A kaleidoscopic mosaic vase inspired this dense and bushy bouquet mingling roses, achillea, and allium flowerheads in a symphony of pinks and yellows. Variegated dogwood foliage and the brilliant fruit and soft green leaves of redcurrants add spice and a touch of whimsy to this lavish arrangement (opposite).

only to watch them at work to realize that, although they may have no formal training, the owners of Mille Feuilles possess a unique and unmistakable talent. Treading a fine line between disciplined restraint and glorious excess, they create innovative and imaginative arrangements in an instantly recognizable style which is all their own. 🌿 Thus for the premiere of Jean-Paul Rappeneau's film Le Hussard sur le toit, they unhesitatingly transformed the famous Parisian restaurant Le Doyen into a typical Provencal house.

This bouquet of pinks, "Sari" roses, peonies, and variegated euonymus was created for the garden festival in the park at Saint-Cloud. With its warm colors, typical of the last days of spring, it seems to herald the arrival of summer.

Commissioned to design every aspect of the launch dinner, they left the private screening with only one idea in mind: to transport all the guests into the luminous, color-filled world of Jean Giono, the French author whose book inspired the film. Tablecloths in red and ochre, saffron-colored crockery, enormous circular buffets lit solely by candlelight, large Anduze pots brimming with sunflowers and olive branches: no detail was overlooked in the creation of this magical evening—even down to the evocative chirping of the cicadas. "When they arrived at Le Doyen that evening, everyone stared wide-eyed in wonder, as though they were children again!" they recall with delight. 🌿 The many visitors to the annual Art du jardin

Made according to an age-old Japanese tradition, the crackle-glazed enameled pots sold in the shop are all unique, and come in an infinite variety of shades.

festival at Saint-Cloud are equally amazed by Mille Feuilles' stand there, conceived as a cosy domestic interior thrown open to inquisitive eyes. From the moment the festival opened in the spring of 1994, the notion caused a sensation. News traveled fast— "Have you seen the Mille Feuilles stand? It's enchanting!"—and visitors crowded to marvel at this astonishing haven, with its skilful balance of intimacy and delicious profusion—furniture with the patina of age, paintings, candlesticks, garden drawings— all wreathed with dried fruits and armfuls of fresh flowers. With their genius for creating interiors, Mille Feuilles could transform even an abandoned factory into a snug and cosy retreat. It is this passion for the spirit of place—almost visceral in its fervor—

that informs each and every one of their arrangements. And it is this same passion that accounts for their fascination with the interiors for which their flowers are destined. If they now enjoy an international reputation, it is because their clients in the four corners of the world, from New York to Tokyo and from Berlin to London or Madrid, know that when they receive their flowers, it will be as though the posy had been chosen by a dear friend who knows them well. This may be a small point, but where flowers are concerned it makes all the difference. ❧ Ten years ago, Mille Feuilles led the way in wrapping their freshly arranged bouquets in open tissue paper in shades chosen to complement the colors of the flowers. "Cellophane has shrink-wrap connotations which filled us with horror," they now admit. "It matters to us that our feelings when composing a bouquet should be transmitted intact to those who have placed their trust in us. We must never forget that flowers are living things and should be treated as such." ❧ This style of wrapping is also perfectly suited to the enduring vogue for posies which has contributed so significantly to the success and reputation of Mille Feuilles. Easy to handle and at home in most vases, posies also provide an opportunity to play more directly with the colors of

A ruff of tissue paper in coordinating colors acts as a foil to this small posy of golden-yellow alstroemerias and lime-green blue pleurum.

flowers, teasing out their harmonies or exploiting their contrasts. While they do not pretend to be behind the growing taste among the public for posies in general, Pierre Brinon and Philippe Landri claim undisputed credit for the invention of posies featuring flowers en masse, with concentrated groups of different sizes within the same composition. This device, which definitively set the seal on their reputation, allows them to explore the aspect of their ephemeral art from which they derive the most enjoyment: the juxtaposition of different textures and

Mille Feuilles accord a place of honor to red flowers—here roses, achillea, and dyed solidaster— with which they create singular and surprising tonal harmonies.

Trailing fronds of foliage such as ivy—a particular favorite of Mille Feuilles—enliven the array of urns and vases that crowds the shop.

Playing delicately on subtle shading and soft curves, this posy combines porcelina roses, achillea, nigella, and the azure spikes of a sheaf of veronica in a timeless and tranquil association (opposite).

colors to create the greatest visual effect. This is also the way they present the flowers in their shop, so that in buying one of these posies, clients are also taking home a small taste of all the sumptuous bouquets on offer. ✿ Whenever possible, Mille Feuilles prefer to obtain their flowers from small nurseries in the area around Paris. A bouquet of blooms grown under glass can never equal the breathtaking flawed grace of naturally grown flowers. "What makes our shop special," explain Pierre Brinon and Philippe Landri, "is the care we devote to seeking out flowers cultivated in small numbers or for their unusual colors." And certainly the flowers in their shop— Renaissance-red scabious, graceful aquilegias, purple-black hellebores, fragrant "Crimson Glory" roses, and humble lupins, to name only a few—seem to carry the scents and breezes of the garden with them in a way that blooms grown under glass never could. But what will they do when these small growers finally disappear? Mille Feuilles dread this all too likely eventuality: it will signify the beginning of the end of a small world in which passion and poetry go hand in hand. ✿ This passion for evoking a particular mood through a play of colors, varying in tones according to the seasons, is both the inspiration and the theme of this book. Glowing with light and color, balancing inspiration with practical advice learned through years of experience, it will intrigue and enchant all those for whom happiness is incomplete without a few flowers. ✿ A bouquet of flowers is a link between our inside world and the world of nature, ephemeral and purely for pleasure in the most delightful way, a luxury available to all. Every season, from spring through winter, possesses its own special éclat, its unique perfumes and treasures. This book guides us through the seasons, shedding fresh light on flowers and foliage, and indicating how to place them in our own interiors, among the furniture and objects that are so personal to us. It is a celebration—how could it not be, when flowers invest everything they touch with a festive air?— and perhaps a consolation, for leafing through these pages one could almost believe that all this fleeting beauty, captured here for an instant, might last for ever.

Chaste white tissue paper—the ultimate in simplicity— provides the perfect foil for this dainty spring nosegay in muted pastel shades.

Spring

A spring collection in a Medici urn sets off the pink-flushed petals of a few boughs of cherry blossom. The dense texture of the tulips, anemones, and bluebells contrasts with the tissue-paper delicacy of the forget-me-nots and sweet peas (above).

Flowing branches of spiraea lend a starry grace to this fragile association of peonies, double tulips, and sweet peas (opposite).

The earth is warmer, the days are longer, and the trees are veiled in fresh new green. Spring is here, and after the interminable gloom of winter, the profusion of color—and especially yellow in every shade—is intoxicating. Narcissi, hyacinths, and tulips, ranunculus, lilac, iris, peonies, and blossom of all sorts provide endless possibilities for arrangements capturing the essence of spring. In our garden in Normandy, the glistening buds on the apple trees burst open, transforming the trees into giant pink-and-white fluffy sheep. With sunshine-yellow forsythia, followed by golden broom, pearly pink cherry blossom, and "snowball" viburnum, they swiftly banish any lingering memories of the grey winter months. Armfuls of parrot tulips and iris, and posies of mixed flowers and foliage are simple but potent ways of celebrating the return of the balmy days of spring. Lavish, airy arrangements of delicate blooms amid clouds of blossom seem to capture the spring sunshine and bring it indoors. After so many weeks of huddling round the fire to ward off the chill of winter, we recklessly fling open doors and windows to welcome in the gentle breezes of spring.

Ranunculus in shades of pastel or sugar pink is a springtime flower par excellence. *Irresistibly charming in tight bud, it grows in luxuriance as its petals unfold (above).*

Freshly picked from our garden, the curvaceous blooms of "Sarah Bernhardt" peonies make a frothy and voluptuous display above a clutch of violet sweet peas (opposite).

All is now bathed in light, whether crystal clear or gauzily soft. Glass vases are the order of the day, letting our greedy eyes feast on slender green stems as though for the first time. For this is a fresh beginning, a time of renewal that seems to bring us a child's youth and vigor. And with the wondering eyes of children, we drink in the gleaming gold of the first crocuses, the soft yellow of primroses and daffodils, and the fathomless blue of dainty forget-me-nots. Meanwhile, with lavish abundance, pearly camellias, cherry blossom, and ranunculus encompass every kind of pink from palest porcelain, through soft pastels, to fuchsia and deep carmine. But no flower seems to celebrate the freshly laundered quality of the spring light better than the peony. Although its glory may be short-lived, it remains the unrivaled queen of the month of May, its frothy blooms lending themselves to voluptuous bouquets which fill the house with their honeyed perfume.

The season of change and renewal, spring is also the time for weddings. No other celebration is so inextricably linked with flowers, from the church to the table for the wedding feast, and from garlands for the bridesmaids to the posy for the bride. Airy and graceful, bridal bouquets are as charming for their symbolic significance as for their delectable prettiness, and may be dried to serve as undying mementoes of a special day that invariably passes in a whirl.

Sadly the springtime is almost equally fleeting. No other season is awaited with such eagerness, and none other passes at such quicksilver speed. All the more reason, then, to celebrate it in all its glorious, albeit ephemeral, abundance.

Sunshine
on a tray

The birds are singing, the sky is a limpid blue, and the light that filters into the room seems to have emerged freshly laundered from the mists of winter. It is impossible to resist flinging the window open and filling your lungs with this sparkling air, laden with subtle, soothing scents. And what could be more delightful, on one of these freshly minted mornings, than breakfast in bed, served on a tray decked with flowers?

What more delightful way to celebrate the return of spring than with breakfast in bed on a sunny Sunday morning? A posy of pansies, sweet peas, and bluebells in dreamy shades of lilac and blue decorates a tray spread with crisp white linen.

PRACTICAL GUIDE

1 The clear colors of this delicate nosegay complement the pastel shades of the porcelain and echo the freshness of the crisp white linen. This type of posy should always be modest in size so that it does not overwhelm the tray.

2 Choose blooms for their fragrance as well as their pretty coloring, so that scent and color combine to electric effect. Pale blue forget-me-nots, glossy purple pansies, faded lilac sweet peas, and lavender bluebells make an irresistible combination, while euphorbia adds pools of golden light to balance the tonality of the composition; and box, with its shiny, prettily rounded leaves, emphasizes its naturalness. If you find the perfume of bluebells too pungent, try replacing them with more delicately scented flowers, such as miniature bunches of grape hyacinths.

3 Choose a small, delicate vase that is sturdy enough not to topple over as you carry the tray. The slightly opaque glass vase used here is an old sugar bowl commandeered for the occasion.

4 Cut the flower stems to length, according to the depth of your vase. Then strip off all leaves that will be below the waterline.

5 Arrange the flowers and foliage in a posy (see p. 143), crossing them far enough along their stems so that the finished posy spills gently over the lip of your container and doesn't either collapse outward or stick bolt upright.

6 Take care to alternate the larger flowers, such as the bluebells and pansies, with the more discreet forget-me-nots and sweet peas. Place the euphorbia and box in the posy to give several evenly distributed pools of light.

7 Once breakfast is finished, the posy would look equally pretty on the bedside table or chest of drawers.

Mother's Day

Bees are not the only creatures attracted to flowers. Children love watching flowers being arranged, triumphantly carrying off discarded blooms—a ranunculus with a broken stem or a tired-looking pansy—as though they were treasures. Why not give them *carte blanche* for once to make their own arrangement? Suggest they make a table decoration for Mother's Day, perhaps—a golden opportunity for them to indulge their creative skills.

The idea is simplicity itself. Yet, easy as this arrangement may be to put together, the glittering reflections of the light on the marbles never fail to produce a bewitching effect.

PRACTICAL GUIDE

1 Give children a transparent dish (round or oblong and not too deep), a bag of clear glass marbles, a bunch of just-opened rosebuds, and a few hyacinth blooms.
2 Many different flowers lend themselves to being used in this way. If you fear the children may prick themselves on the roses, use fully open anemones instead. Whatever your choice of flowers, make sure that there is a contrast—but not a clash—of colors in order to avoid any risk of monotony. Here, the delicate mauve of the hyacinths was chosen to complement the glowing yellow of "Princess Michael of Kent" roses.

3 Guide the children in the right direction but be careful not to interfere: budding landscape gardeners must be allowed to feel that this is *their* achievement.
4 Let them fill the container with water, then gently pile in the marbles to a depth of about one inch. Help them carefully detach the individual hyacinth flowers from the central stem, then float them on the surface of the water. Finally, cut the stems from the roses and float them among the hyacinths. The masterpiece is ready! Now all they need do is arrange the flowers evenly.

Creating a pretty arrangement for Mother's Day can give children enormous pleasure. In this simple and sparkling table decoration, dewy spring flowers and clear glass marbles combine to magical effect.

May birthday tea

May is the month of lilies-of-the-valley, the diminutive, intoxicatingly perfumed member of the lily family without which springtime is incomplete. In France, children still follow the charming tradition of offering their mothers gifts of lily-of-the-valley on May Day, but for the rest of the month their exquisite little blooms tend to be overlooked. In the ten years since we opened Mille Feuilles, we have made it our mission to demonstrate how to include into mixed bouquets this ravishing flower with its tremulous white bells.

Whatever the dominant tones, its milky whiteness blends in perfectly, adding flair and a touch of cheer—for it is after all the traditional symbol of happiness. And at a time when the colors of the garden are in a state of ferment—with yellows deepening, roses veering to crimson, and greens shedding the filmy transparency of early spring—this versatility is all the more valuable. This posy of flowers for a birthday tea-table in May seems to welcome the spring sunshine as a guest of honor at

Posies are a favorite decoration for parties: here, with their fresh spring colors, they bring a dash of high spirits and refreshing simplicity to a birthday tea-table (opposite).

the table. The opaque glass vase we have chosen echoes the floral motif.

PRACTICAL GUIDE

1 The golden rule for all posies intended as table decorations is that they should be low enough for guests to be able to see over the top of them: if the guests are too busy peering round them, they are unlikely to stop to admire them! If the party is a large one, why not make a number of identical posies and tuck them between the place settings? The overall effect will be of a dazzling ribbon of flowers stretching the length of the table, which cannot fail to delight your guests.

2 Choose flowers that are unerringly fresh in color and delicately perfumed, with—if you include lily-of-the-valley— a note of bewitching sophistication. In these posies, its delicate bells serve to mediate between the glowing colors of apricot-yellow "Princess Michael of Kent" roses and salmon-pink pansies. Their pearly whiteness also highlights the green of the just-opening flowers of a "snowball" viburnum and contrasts softly with the yellow-fringed foliage of variegated euonymus, dark as box.

3 Strip the roses of their thorns (see p. 141), and remove any leaves which might cloud the water.

4 Then arrange the blooms into posies, following the advice on page 143.

The tremulously romantic bells of lily-of-the-valley lend a special charm to these posies of roses, pansies, and "snowball" viburnum, designed to be small enough to tuck in between each place setting (below).

Romantic bouquet

The studio where we make our bouquets lies between the workshop and the garden shed. We chose a glass vase for this confection, in which

the faded mauve of the lilac blooms and the sumptuous snowy whiteness of the peonies are lent zest by the sharper tones of ranunculus, rhododendrons, and sweet peas (above and opposite).

Somewhere buried deep, most people treasure a memory scented with the evocative honey fragrance of lilac. Lilac is the romantic flower *par excellence*, equally at home invading humble cottage gardens as it is propping itself up against the elegant walls of imposing mansions. One of lilac's principal charms is its spontaneity, and this is the quality we set out to celebrate in this mixed bouquet. In its complete freedom and naturalness, this bouquet has the poetry and careless charm of the gardens we love best.

PRACTICAL GUIDE

1 Among the countless lilac varieties available, our preference is for mauve or violet shades. Our "Katherine Havemeyer," planted four years ago, rewards us each spring with a mass of double pale violet flowers, deliciously perfumed. Do not hesitate to grow deep purple lilacs with "Charles de Gaulle" or "Paul Neyron" roses, which will echo them with their washed-out mauves, creating a breathtaking composition of petals of different textures, all seemingly dipped in the same powdery velvet dye. White lilac, for us, lacks the sensuality and softness of the purple shades, and moreover has the unfortunate habit of sprouting spots of rust after the first shower of rain. If you should find

yourself in the region of Honfleur, on France's Atlantic coast, in springtime, you may be as surprised as we once were to be offered bunches of pale yellow lilac by market stall holders. You will scour the florists' shops in vain for this variety, dubbed "Primrose."

Toward the end of winter, wholesalers offer a greenhouse lilac which may be more resistant, but which does not have the suppleness, the volume, or anything like the charm of garden varieties.

2 To add zest to the mauve sprays of "Maréchal Foch" lilac use a bunch of sweet peas in a variety of colors, including a range of exhilarating citrus and orange tones. The pink of the rhododendrons contributes their more sophisticated charm, but the pivotal role in achieving the right balance between light and dark goes to the frothy, creamy white of the peonies. Ranunculus punctuates the bouquet with its pastel-colored pompons, marking a discreet transition between the rich lilac clusters, the sumptuous peonies, and the tenderly fragile petals of the sweet peas.

3 Lilac is equally magnificent on its own, with languid armfuls drooping nonchalantly in heavy containers, like dense, frothy shrubs.

4 Lilac does not enjoy a long life once cut. To make it last as long as possible, it is essential to crush the stems with a hammer (see p. 141). This enables the stems to take up water, and prevents a scar from forming over the cut—a common reason for the premature fading of cut lilac.

5 Arrange the posy (see p. 143), taking care to position the lilac on the fringes of the bouquet, where its clusters have room to cascade gracefully.

Springtime abundance

The first rays of the spring sun are an irresistible invitation to indulgence. Forget restraint and moderation, and surrender to temptation: pluck a rose here, a spray of blossom there, and perhaps a few pansies, and soon you will have a bouquet as fresh as a spring morning.

PRACTICAL GUIDE

1 The airy, luminous arrangement shown here seems to spill out of its container with careless abandon, but the flowers used—pearly roses, lilac-colored pansies, pink-and-white apple blossom, and the tiny pink-and-white stars of *Viburnum* "Anne Russell"—have been chosen to create a delicious sense of balance and an overall softness of tone. The variegated leaves of euonymus and dogwood are tempered, meanwhile, by the more discreet velvety grey foliage of *Cineraria maritima*.

2 For this very dense type of arrangement we recommend using blocks of synthetic foam, available from florists and garden centers. It is essential to prepare the foam correctly (see p. 142).

3 Choose a broad, shallow container such as a basket, jardiniere, or tureen for a low composition such as this. Here a zinc-lined Napoleon III "woven" basket makes an ideal receptacle for this display of freshly opened blooms.

4 To ensure maximum penetration into the foam, cut the flower stems diagonally as short as possible. Strip the roses of their thorns with a knife blade (see p. 141).

5 Poke the stems into the foam one by one, starting with the foliage, which lends volume and density to the bouquet. A prettily twisted branch may even dictate the direction of the entire composition.

6 The charm of this bouquet lies in the sense of curiosity it excites. Its intriguing effect is produced by concentrating the flowers in small bunches of a single variety, so exploiting to the full the contrasts between them.

7 Arrange the masses at different depths to add relief and shadows to the bouquet; this seems to reveal new secrets with every glance.

8 Display the arrangement on a low table, so that its silken delicacy may be admired from above.

Still in bud or softly unfolding, spring flowers grouped lavishly in a low basket seem to celebrate the gentle warmth of an April morning. Placed in front of a window, this diaphanous arrangement seems to draw the garden into the house (above).

Spring finds its essence in translucent white petals, flushed with pink, and the most delicate of roses. Here their laciness is echoed by a dainty white-painted Napoleon III basket (opposite).

Tulips
and euphorbias

Two varieties of parrot tulip and a lime-yellow cloud of euphorbia together compose a shimmering ode to spring. The season's unrivaled queens of the garden, tulips have a unique ability to continue their sinuous growth after they have been cut, thus creating

graceful arrangements which change day by day (above and opposite).

No flower better symbolizes the return of spring than the tulip. A native of Turkey, from the sixteenth century it was cultivated by the Dutch, who concocted an inexhaustible variety of colors and shapes. The petals may be pale or dark, plain or variegated, round or elegantly elongated, smooth or ruffled, even extravagantly fringed in the case of parrot tulips, and form single or double blooms which vie with each other in elegance. Their pearly whiteness is the acme of purity, their yellows glow like the sun, and their flame colors are simply irresistible.

It would be a crime to neglect this paragon of flowers—rustic and simple when short-stemmed, urbane and sophisticated on long, sinuous stems— which, among its many other virtues, lasts well in water from March to May. So perfect that it is hard to believe it is quite real, it even confounds us by continuing to grow after it has been cut. A bouquet of tulips is constantly changing, arranging itself from day to day: these are flowers that know their own minds, and any attempt to persuade them otherwise is futile.

PRACTICAL GUIDE

1 In this arrangement, orange and deep pink "Apricot Parrot" and "Flaming Parrot" tulips combine with bracts of euphorbia (*E. cyparissias*) to create a shimmering firework display of color.
2 Choose a transparent vase to reveal the tulips' graceful stems.
3 As tulips keep on growing after they have been cut, it is important to cut their stems shorter than those of other flowers, so that they do not tower over the others. In a tied posy, the tulips will at first appear slightly sunken within the arrangement, but will soon grow to the same height as the others.
4 Strip off the leaves below the waterline, retaining those closer to the flowers so that they punctuate the bouquet with their elegant curves.
5 Plunge the euphorbia into a bucket of water (see p. 141) to prevent the sap in the stems from harming the other flowers.
6 In a bouquet consisting solely of tulips, you can prevent the flowers from flopping by filling the container to only one-third of its depth, then topping it up as necessary without changing the water. When tulips are mixed with other flowers, as here, a few copper coins in the bottom of the vase should stop them from collapsing.
7 Make a posy, following the advice on page 143.
8 As tulips generally need a day or two to settle before looking their best, it is wise to arrange bouquets such as this well in advance.

Tulip vase

The wonderfully aesthetic tulip vase is one flower container that should be displayed to full advantage. Contemporary or antique, these ingenious vases are equally decorative whether or not they are filled with flowers. Here, the blue tones of Chinese porcelain take on a deeper intensity in the company of the subtle ivory petals of elegant miniature tulips.

In the sixteenth century, when the Dutch introduced the tulip to Europe, a new type of vase was created in order to display the beauties of this fabulous new flower from Turkey. The tulip vase consisted of a cluster of small containers, frequently pyramidal in shape, arranged so that two or three stems might be slipped into each. Long-stemmed tulips are best displayed in tall, obelisk-shaped tulip vases, sadly now rarely found outside antique shops. The few examples that we have been lucky enough to find—and the modern versions in both porcelain and terracotta that we sell in our shop—have always been enthusiastically received by our clients. This is hardly surprising, given the rare ability of these tulip vases to combine practicality with extreme elegance.

PRACTICAL GUIDE

1 The client who brought us this Chinese porcelain tulip vase, with a description of its Vermeer-inspired setting, was possibly a touch surprised when we suggested simply filling it with ivory-colored tulips. But pale flowers can be at their most effective in a somber setting, providing that they are sufficiently substantial to ensure that any light is reflected by their petals, as though radiating from them. The blue of Chinese porcelain, moreover, responds well to the presence of white, which serves to accentuate and intensify it.

2 The proportions of these small tulips, with their long, creamy flowers, are perfect. The success of a composition such as this depends on establishing just the right balance between the vase itself and the flowers it contains.

3 There is no reason why tulip vases should be reserved exclusively for tulips. All flowers with serpentine stems which slowly meander as the blooms open are suitable: "Mona Lisa" anemones, ranunculus, and—best of all—small poppies look particularly ravishing.

4 Whichever flowers you choose, remember to arrange them the day before, so that they have time to settle down.

Symphony
in pink and yellow

With flowers as with people, opposites attract, and the most unlikely partnerships can sometimes be the most successful ones. Often, flowers that could hardly be more different in shape, texture, or color work particularly well together. In this little nosegay, the deep pink satiny pompons of ranunculus combine with greenish-yellow bracts of euphorbia to create spectacular contrasts of texture and color.

PRACTICAL GUIDE

1 The exquisite blooms of ranunculus are available in a wide range of colors—always even, never dappled or variegated—from the palest tones to the deepest. The variety used here, "Victoria," has slightly larger flowers than the ordinary variety. These spring flowers are cultivated under glass in winter so that their fresh colors are always available to brighten dull days. Their one slight drawback is the stems' tendency to flop, which means that they need to be supported by other flowers or foliage.
2 The vivid colors of the arrangement call for a simple glass vase, leaving the green of the stems visible as a restful point of transition for the eye (see following pages).
3 Remove the ranunculus leaves, which are not especially attractive, but keep the buds, which draw the eye and add a note of extravagance.

4 It is often useful to have ready a reserve container (a florist's bucket, for example) in which to plunge flower stems for a few hours before arranging them. Some species, for example euphorbia and daffodils, secrete a sap from their stems which can prove harmful to other flowers, and so this step is indispensable.
5 Make a posy (see p. 143).

A sheaf of broom seems to light up the workshop in which we make our arrangements, its sunny colors echoing the euphorbia bracts in the neat little nosegay.

In their startling freshness, spring flowers prompt some unexpected associations. The flamboyance of this partnership of saturated pink ranunculus and lime-yellow euphorbia is discreetly aided by a simple glass vase and the restful green of the flower stems.

Broom, cherry blossom, and weeping willow

Spring flowers—real and ceramic—conspire to confuse (below).

Freshly cut sprays of broom make a splash of luminous yellow, their sculptural outlines softened by trailing fronds of weeping willow (opposite). Bouquets on this bold scale are best arranged in situ.

*I*n spring, fruit trees and flowering shrubs transform any garden into a symphony of luminous color. On country walks or a stroll round the garden, for those lucky enough to have one, it is impossible to resist plucking a few boughs of apple blossom, hawthorn, or lilac to brighten up the house.

PRACTICAL GUIDE

1 The selection you make will be decided by taste and opportunity. As a general rule, the structure and delicacy of boughs of blossom are such that they do not need to be mixed with other species. Here, however, the distinctive shape of sprays of broom, at once sculptural and nonchalantly unkempt, gave us the idea of partnering them with trusses of cherry blossom, the glossy foliage of *Prunus padus*, and trailing strands of willow, whose graceful almond-green curves provide the link between the bouquet and its setting.

2 For bouquets such as this, if possible choose blossom that is still in bud, so that you can enjoy its brief life to the full. The buds of cherry blossom, almond blossom, and spiraea make such a spectacular sight as they open out, moreover, that it would be a shame to miss it.

3 Arrangements of flowering branches dictate a departure from our habitual springtime choice of transparent containers, as they need weighty receptacles, perhaps of cast iron or, as here, enameled earthenware. Sober colors and slender shapes show off the structure of the branches to best advantage, while tall, straight-sided containers help to disguise and flatter any stiffness.

4 It is wise to create large arrangements *in situ* to help avoid the delicate blossom on the branches being overhandled, while also giving you the opportunity to decide on the proportions of the bouquet as you go along.

5 Before starting on the arrangement of the bouquet, prepare the branches by crushing the ends with a hammer (see p. 141). This enables them to take up water and prevents a scar from forming over the cut.

6 Owing to the weight of the boughs and their unwieldy nature it is essential to anchor them somehow, either with a classic flower-holder of the kinds available in the shops, or with a home-made version fashioned from a square of chicken wire, molded to the shape of the vase and weighted down inside the vase if necessary with pebbles (see p. 141).

7 Then insert the branches one by one, starting with the stiffest ones, in this case the cherry blossom. Place the flowing weeping willow tresses last of all to add movement to the finished composition.

Center stage

We make no secret of our belief that flowers are an integral part of any decorative scheme. But whether they are the stars of the occasion or play a more discreet supporting role, they must possess the power to intrigue and surprise. Over the years, our window displays have caught the attention of a number of clients who now habitually ask us to style rooms for receptions or intimate dinner parties.

In these ephemeral designs, our primary aim is to establish the closest possible rapport between an unfamiliar world and the flowers arranged within it, to the point where inanimate and animate—or vegetable—objects seem to complement and conspire with each other in a relationship of mutually rewarding complicity.

In this rather monumental decor, we were attracted by the unfinished surfaces and flaking eclecticism of the woodwork and stone walls, which called for a similarly crude, raw approach. The sea green of the varnished earthenware Medici urn creates a contrast with the

dominant tones of the room and fixes the attention. Our impromptu approach was to create height with blossom-laden boughs, exhilarating in their freshness.

PRACTICAL GUIDE

1 In spring, the choice of flowering plants is overwhelming. Lilac, golden-yellow forsythia, softly stylized cherry and almond blossom, apple blossom, Japanese quince after the last frosts, and all the viburnums, including the popular "snowball" variety, together offer an almost infinite variety of color and perfume. Here we chose boughs of pear blossom for the lavish spontaneity of their habit, the exquisite delicacy of their coloring, and the perfection of the soft green stamens within each flower.

2 Medici urns and their shallower Chambord cousins were traditionally used as decorative features in gardens and gateways, massed with annuals and pierced underneath for drainage. For interior use, they need to be either lined with a watertight container or filled with pre-soaked synthetic foam—our choice for this arrangement.

3 Place the branches in the urn one by one. In wide-necked containers such as this, place the tallest and straightest branches to the top and slightly to the back. Shorter, more supple branches then add fullness and lightness to the sides and foreground.

Urns of herculean proportions are equally well suited to low, extremely compact arrangements. Here, a cushion of "snowball" viburnum and ranunculus complements an imposing container rather than competing with it. Picked while still in bud, the snowball flowers of the viburnum are a refreshing acid green, highlighting the clear orange and pink splashes of the ranunculus (above).

The inimitable grace of a simple bouquet of pear blossom would look equally distinguished in a contemporary interior. With time, a shower of petals will cascade in soft drifts on to the pedestal, creating an ephemeral composition of bewitching, Japanese-inspired charm (opposite).

Chaste whiteness

Glass vases are particularly well suited to tulips, their transparency displaying the flowers' elegantly curvaceous stems to full advantage (below).

No meditation on the subject of flowers would be complete without a hymn to the virtues of white. To the ancient Greeks and Romans, white symbolized innocence and chastity, in Asia and the Far East it is the color of mourning, and Christianity has adopted it to celebrate the rituals of happiness—weddings, christenings, and first communions—of which it is now the indispensable symbol and accessory. A bouquet of white flowers invariably combines elegance, style, and freshness. White flowers come in a thousand different shades, some tinged with amber, others so ethereally translucent that you wonder whether they are not merely a trick of the light. Among the purest of white flowers—powerful in their fascination and so flawless that they hardly seem real—are light and insubstantial cosmos, fresh-petaled camellias, and porcelain-perfect orchids.

PRACTICAL GUIDE

1 This posy subtly partners the green-flushed white of roses and the creamier tones of peonies with the lemon-white of sweet peas and the snowy mass of double tulips. The whole extravaganza is set against a cloud of starry white spiraea, which adds movement and frothy lightness to the bouquet. Fronds of box, meanwhile, serve to emphasize the different nuances of white while dispelling any risk of monotony.

2 If possible, choose a glass vase on a stem for this arrangement: it enhances the effect of limpid translucency, with the light shimmering in silver reflections, and allows supple-stemmed flowers to cascade gracefully. The narrow neck of the vase provides good support for the arrangement, while its height lends balance.

3 Remove all leaves from the base of the stems, and strip the roses of their thorns.

4 Then make the posy by crossing the stems and rotating the bouquet as it grows (see p. 143).

5 With its neutral tones, this posy would look well anywhere—bearing in mind only that the lighter its position, the more luminous its whites will gleam.

Richly colored flowers may inspire associations of brilliant flamboyance, but the pure light of spring calls for the shimmering though infinitely subtle reflections and variations of a bouquet of white flowers (opposite).

Bless the bride

Of all life's celebrations, weddings more than any other seem to demand the presence of armfuls of flowers. It is as if the joy of the happy couple is captured in their wedding flowers—so that all may share in it. Appearing in the church and at the reception, as well as being carried by the bride herself and her bridesmaids, wedding flowers are a river of joy running through a wedding celebration, inviting people to join in the happy mood. The freshness of flowers represents new love, new life.

RESTRAINED ELEGANCE

For the marriage ceremony illustrated on this page, the couple opted for a restrained approach, based on a palette of white with touches of blue, with romantic clouds of gypsophila setting the keynote.

PRACTICAL GUIDE

1 Easy to work with, happy out of water, light and airy, the filigree branches of gypsophila can be teased into virtually any shape desired.
2 Tie posies on to the end of each pew with white tulle, to emphasize the snowy whiteness of the starry flowers, and stud them with butterflies made from blue feathers.
3 Decorate the altar and chandeliers with billowing clouds of gypsophila to echo the pure white of the bridal gown.

COUNTRY ABUNDANCE

The table decorations for the feast at this wedding in a Normandy *auberge* (see following page), exude softness and abundance in a fragrant ribbon of flowers threading its way down the length of the table. Points of intense color provide rhythm and depth, as soft pink peonies and blushing sweet peas combine with smoldering mauves, rich roses, buttercup-yellow alchemilla, and the fresh green of fronds of raspberry, studded with unripe fruit. Watered satin ribbons peep out from between the flowers, bringing a foreshortening effect and an additional note of softness.

PRACTICAL GUIDE

1 To be successful, an arrangement such as this must observe three basic rules: to be not too tall, not too highly perfumed, and not too cumbersome.
2 Arrange the flowers in pre-soaked synthetic foam before bringing them to the table, where you can add the final touches and mask the foam with flowers and foliage. You may even do this the day before, in order to give the flowers time to unfold overnight and reveal their full beauty.

Billowing white clouds of gypsophila, light as air and able to survive out of water, are anchored to pew ends

and chandeliers, creating the illusion of an avenue of wild flowers leading the bride and groom to the altar (opposite and above).

When creating the decor for weddings, we like to associate pastel colors with bolder tones. The sumptuous ribbon of flowers running the length of the marriage table serves as a link between the bridal couple and each of their guests (above and right).

BRIDAL BOUQUET

The bride's posy must be pretty, needless to say, but that is not all. Designed to complement her gown in every detail, it also has to fulfil certain practical requirements. Too heavy, and it becomes a burden; too long, and it is difficult to carry gracefully; too much pollen, especially of the staining variety, and the consequences for delicate organdy, silk, and lace can only be imagined. Compact nosegays are therefore the most popular and practical choice, with the emphasis on "clean" flowers.

PRACTICAL GUIDE

1 Small camomile roses, pale yellow alchemilla, spires of white perennial sweet peas, variegated euonymus, and the delicate ivory-colored umbels of asclepias combine to create a delicately balanced palette of neutral tones, emphasized by the filmy length of iridescent ribbon with which it is tied.
2 Assemble the flowers as in a classic posy (see p. 143), massing the roses in bunches of four or five in order to draw the eye to their soft pearly tones. Clean all the flower stems, remove the rose thorns, and tie the composition together tightly with string in order to make it easier to hold. The ribbon is purely decorative, serving to camouflage the string.
3 A bouquet may be dried after the ceremony. Hang it upside down in a warm, dry place for two or three weeks to become an everlasting memento of this special day.

4 Lilies, symbol of purity and a perfect accessory to the splendor of white satin or crepe, are often requested at weddings. If they are to be used, take special care to remove their stamens, laden with brilliant orange pollen which transfers liberally—and frequently indelibly—on to everything it brushes against.

Practical and aesthetic considerations combine in the wedding posy, designed to complement the bride's gown. Not too large, not too heavy, and without too much pollen, it may be dried as an everlasting memento (opposite).

Summer

For the sake of a few hours of pleasure savoring their bewitching honey fragrance, we can rarely resist the temptation to steal a few cascades of purple wisteria flowers from the old wall of the house (above).

A vase gleaned from a second-hand shop in Antibes holds an incandescent arrangement including roses, phlox, hypericum, clematis, and penstemon in shades of gold and crimson (opposite).

Invariably too short in temperate regions, summer is nevertheless the embodiment of the sun itself, a beacon of light and glowing heat around which the other seasons orbit like satellite planets. Spring paves the way for it, fall remembers it with lingering pleasure, and winter longs for it with wistful nostalgia. Now the sun warms the land, the evenings are long, and nature seems to conspire with all our desires. Even time, that fugitive which so often escapes us, seems to shrug off its customary haste and slip into the languid rhythm of long, glorious days. From dawn to miraculously late dusk, it presents a spectacle of constantly unfolding delights.

In the garden, flowers vie with each other in splendor and intoxicating fragrance. Cascading wisteria, misty scabious, and a multitude of roses together form set-pieces of romantic profusion; dazzling zinnias and flamboyant nasturtiums make exhilarating contrasts with lupins and delphiniums of deepest blue; while diaphanous sweet peas, wine-dark achillea, and voluptuous clusters of phlox make spectacular partnerships with graceful aquilegias and trailing clematis. Infinitely varied in both shape and color, the flowers of summer make this the most prodigal of all the seasons. The summer palette, more intense than that of spring, also covers a broader spectrum. The spires of delphiniums and antirrhinums mingle luxuriantly with magnificent roses, spiky thistles, and ethereal nigella. Now more than ever is the time to risk daring contrasts and provocative combinations. Do not be fainthearted in arranging marriages of opposites, whether of shape or color. While foliage may play a less prominent part than in other seasons, it now acquires a new density which serves to highlight certain colors and to lend volume to bouquets which might otherwise be too dainty. Variegated foliage,

from hostas to dogwood and euonymus, and the blue-grey leaves of some varieties of willow meanwhile add an airy grace to arrangements on a more imposing scale.

With the blossoming of summer, the translucency of spring gives way to a velvety opaqueness, a drowsy heaviness of petals and foliage enfolding bewitching effects of light and shade. The house windows are thrown open, and as a profound harmony evolves between the inside and outside worlds, the boundaries between them melt away. Reflecting this mood, summer bouquets are microcosms of this rich profusion—to the bemusement of the occasional itinerant bee.

Vases for springtime bouquets tend toward transparency. Summer blooms call for simple, unsophisticated containers, often borrowed from the kitchen or the garden shed: metal boxes, painted pitchers, earthenware jugs, and, above all, zinc in every size and shape, from milk churns to battered watering cans.

And while the first fine days of spring are a persuasive argument for breakfast in bed, our favorite meal at this hottest time of year is undoubtedly lunch. The ephemeral decoration of a table set in the perfumed shade of tall lime trees and scattered with peaches and roses has a paradoxically timeless charm.

At the height of summer the long, languorous days merge in a drowsy haze that promises to last for ever. But now is the time to garner some of the generosity of these halcyon days in anticipation of darker times to come, making posies and globes of dried flowers to bring warmth and light in the winter months. Now, above all, is the time simply to enjoy the all too short-lived colors and perfumes of nature at its most lavishly extravagant.

Scabious, lisianthus (eustoma), carrot flowers, oats, and variegated ivy combine to create a cool, refreshing bouquet on a theme of white and translucent green (above).

"In the language of gardeners," wrote Julien Green, "plants die, but roses expire." A cluster of curvaceous shell-pink "Pierre de Ronsard" roses, spilling out of their vase in a sunny window, captures the fleeting, voluptuous beauty of full-blown summer roses (opposite).

Country cousins

If flowers had moods, zinnias would be all jaunty cheerfulness. Whatever variety you choose, a posy of zinnias invariably seems to radiate energy and zest for life. With dahlias and nasturtiums, they share a clear, concentrated palette as fresh as summer fruits, guaranteed to brighten the house even on stormy days. Their sturdy, healthy blooms, in uncompromising shades from flamboyant red to citrus yellow, Tyrian

purple, and electric orange, seem calculated to inspire painters and dispel shadows.

Easy and unfussy to cultivate, they still find their place in old-fashioned cottage gardens, and it is always a pleasure to glimpse them, perky spots of color perched on fleshy stems, peeping out from between the rows of lettuces and runner beans.

PRACTICAL GUIDE

1 Cut the flowers in the cool of the morning or evening, taking care afterward to remove any leaves from the parts of the stems which will be under water.

2 For a small and informal posy like this, choose an improvised vase such as this nicely tarnished old metal jam pot, whose golds and ambers form a splendidly emphatic partnership with the sharp colors of the zinnias.

3 Make a posy (see p. 143), teasing over the lip of the vase a generous ruff of tough little leaves. These set off both the exuberance of the open blooms and the curious shape of the buds, like tiny clenched fists.

4 Regularly top up the vase with water to keep it looking fresh for a week or more.

Jaunty zinnias in a Fauvist palette of saturated reds, yellows, purples, and oranges radiate zest and lend their sparkle to an old jam pot, neatly demonstrating that the simplest arrangements are sometimes the most effective.

Nosegays
of nasturtiums

A garden flower *par excellence*, the nasturtium has the gift of transforming hedges, low walls, and lanky bushes with its graceful cascades of flaming color. Generations of children have used its large, round leaves as dolls' plates, and they would doubtless be even more delighted to know that the flowers may be eaten, lending their refreshing, peppery taste and brilliant looks to summer salads.

A native of Peru, the prolific nasturtium flowers in every shade of yellow and orange, with recent varieties adding a fiery blood red to its palette. Its slender leaf and flower stems, intertwined and apparently fragile as glass, are always ready to pop up in places where you least expect expect them.

PRACTICAL GUIDE

1 Simple enough for a child to make, little bouquets of nasturtiums derive their charm from the natural movement inherent in the flowers' structure: just put them in a vase, and they will do the rest.

2 In the house, nasturtiums seem to have an instinctive affinity with anything blue, their blazing oranges and yellows serving to intensify and stimulate cooler tones. In this arrangement (see following pages), a collection of stoneware pots in the colors of tropical seas and an indigo-colored wall make a dramatic foil to a group of diminutive but dramatic nosegays. Three vases of different shapes and heights are linked by the flowers themselves on their long, inquisitive stems, which seem ever on the point of clambering from one vase to another.

3 The dark green of ivy makes a magnificent foil to the brilliance of nasturtiums.

4 Make small nosegays (see p. 143), tie them once, then surround them with ivy leaves and bind them again to produce a ravishing effect.

To improvise a table decoration, why not simply scatter nasturtiums and French marigolds over a brightly colored cloth? The stronger the colors, the more striking the effect will be.

Two or three small nosegays are all you need to bring to life a collection of pots and vases, such as this glazed stoneware. A dazzling handful of nasturtiums, plucked straight from the garden and arranged informally without further ado, instantly electrifies the composition, lending it a clean-edged, contemporary feel.

Cascades
of greenery

Bouquets of a single color are often the most restful to contemplate. In this green arrangement, the effects of light, texture, and contour have been called into play to add drama and interest, and avoid any danger of blandness. Within a single color, nature offers an infinity of rich tones and subtle shades which we only need to be adventurous enough to play with.

For centuries green was believed to be the color of fate, symbolizing both good and bad fortune. While in medieval iconology yellow-green signified abject despair, for many people nowadays it is a color of hope and renewal. This was the inspiration for the bouquet shown here, with its triumphant exuberance standing as a defiant challenge to the fleeting nature of time. In its lushness and luminosity it will lighten the darkest corner for many long, summer days.

PRACTICAL GUIDE

1 A green bouquet is in fact a combination of any number of greens, from the pale yellow-green of moluccella (also known as shell flower or bells of Ireland) to the blue-green of allium and poppy seedheads, themselves far removed from the rusty grey-green of the cascading panicles of pennisetum. The curious inflorescences also give off a subtle fragrance of vetiver, further adding to the charms of this bouquet.
2 Occasionally, a container provides the inspiration for the bouquet it holds. In this unusually apposite instance, the green fronds seem to cascade like a fountain from the handsome terracotta water filter which serves as a vase, the liquid translucency of the moluccella bells contributing to the illusion.
3 Period containers such as this may be porous and therefore unsuitable for holding water. If this is the case, simply place a bucket or similar recipient inside it and fill this with pre-soaked synthetic foam.
4 Then anchor the different species of flowers and seedheads in the foam, setting them close together to emphasize their contrasting textures and shapes. Place the stems of moluccella and pennisetum first, to create the necessary density for this luxuriant display.
5 Take care to water the arrangement regularly to keep the synthetic foam moist.

For this lush green display, we chose the seedheads of allium and poppies, the arching panicles of pennisetum, and a single species of flower: moluccella, with its astonishing pale bells that seem to hold the light. In combination, all these different greens conspire to produce a mysterious, vertiginous effect (left and opposite).

Wild oats
and roses

We enjoy unexpected associations and bold contrasts. Here, delicate roses—the soul of the garden—and rustic oats are combined in a low bouquet symbolic of harvest-time and abundance (below and opposite).

Using fruits of the field as well as the garden, this bouquet mingles whiskery oats with several varieties of rose in a subtle combination of fragrances. The roses, plucked at random according to fancy, offer a delicate pot-pourri of colors, from the pale apricot of "Ambiance" to the shell pink of "Pierre de Ronsard," with richer tones added by "Crimson Glory" and the carmine blooms of a rose which was already in the garden when we arrived, and which obstinately refuses to reveal its identity. The oats from a neighboring field punctuate the composition with their aromatic spikes.

PRACTICAL GUIDE

1 Some varieties of rose—"Nevada," for instance, with its pale green leaves, most rugosas, and *R. webbiana* with its delicate blue-green foliage—have highly decorative, serrated leaves in pretty shades of green. After the stems have been shortened for a bouquet, any spare leafy parts may be slipped in between the blooms to create a natural effect.
2 If you choose a shallow, wide container such as this zinc basin, fill it with fine chicken wire to hold and support your flowers and foliage.
3 Strip off the lower leaves and thorns from the roses, retaining any attractive foliage. Cut the flower stems diagonally to help them take up water.
4 If the heat has made your roses droop before you arrange them, revive them by plunging their stems into boiling water for a couple of minutes (taking care to shield the blooms from the steam), then plunge them in cold water. This helps to remove air bubbles which prevent water from reaching the flowers.
5 Then pack the basin with the stems of the oats and roses, mingling them closely together. Use flowers of different sizes, and alternate buds with open blooms to help create the feeling of a bouquet freshly gathered from the garden.
6 Designed to be admired from all sides, this arrangement would sit well on a low table.

Three vases
in monochrome

One of summer's simple pleasures: filling all the containers in the house with artless posies straight from the garden. The fun of this approach lies in playing with colors like a painter, mixing and matching them to suit your mood or fancy.

This neat and simple composition of bright colors and unfussy shapes is both restful and refreshing. Striking crimson pinks in a blue beaded glass vase draw the eye to both the sulphurous yellow achillea beside them and the subtler slate blue of the echinops below. These uncompromising color contrasts are tempered by a choice of wide-necked vases, all in stained-glass shades of blue. The color of the sky and the sea, blue has the ability to be both warm and cooling, invigorating and soothing.

PRACTICAL GUIDE

1 Soft blue grape hyacinths, flame-red dwarf tulips, and luminous yellow wild daffodils make a spectacular combination, for example: a simple way of celebrating the end of winter which children would enjoy helping with.
2 Jam jars make gloriously simple vases for similar displays of summer flowers.
3 Remove all the leaves, and cut the stems diagonally to help them take up water. Then make each posy (see p. 143).
4 What better place for this trim arrangement than the bathroom, as here, or perhaps a passageway or corridor?

A basket of flowers

Achilleas form a large family of hardy perennials, the most familiar of which bear their masses of tiny flowers in densely packed heads. In the garden they tend to be invasive, and it is virtually *de rigueur* to divide the plants every two or three years.

Here, a few clumps of dusty pink achillea have been untangled in order to fill a gently bleached basket to overflowing, their old-fashioned coloring recalling the faded charm of old houses in which time seems to stand still.

PRACTICAL GUIDE

1 A similar bouquet composed exclusively of yellow flowerheads would be equally appealing in a completely different way, with the ageing flowers recalling the colors of the dying sun.
2 If you choose to display your arrangement in a basket, line it first with a glass vase, as nearly as possible mirroring the shape of the basket.
3 Clean the stems of the achillea to avoid the danger of leaves rotting in the water and creating bad smells.
4 Then mass the flowerheads together to make a plump cushion. Shorten their stems to make the bouquet look like a *trompe-l'œil* cover to the basket.
5 To stay fresh achilleas need a lot of water, so you will need to top up the arrangement at regular intervals.

6 However, if you simply stop replenishing the water the bouquet will slowly dry. Achilleas do not wilt as they dry, and lose very little of their intensity of color, so they make a most attractive dried arrangement. Thus preserved, the bouquet will serve as a reminder of the summer's warmth on chilly winter days.
7 This bouquet would suit a corridor or passageway. Owing to their distinctive aroma, achilleas are not suitable for use in bedrooms or small, confined spaces.

Massed in a wicker basket, these achilleas already seem impervious to the passing of time. Very easy to dry, they will remain virtually unchanged through the winds of fall and the snows of winter.

After the deluge

This improvised bouquet, picked in our garden after a rainstorm, found a perfect home in a pretty Wedgwood milk jug in just the right shade of blue.

Gardeners view an approaching storm with mounting trepidation. Heavy showers make short work of fragile flower stems, and in their aftermath herbaceous borders all too often present a pathetic scene of drooping stems, drenched blooms, and ripped petals. Invariably a solitary campanula or rose bravely raises its head above the surrounding carnage.

The garden's loss may be the flower-arranger's gain, however. This is the ideal moment to dust off vases languishing in the back of cupboards and fill them with refugees from the storm. Here, a blue Wedgwood milk jug has become home to a collection of mauve and white blooms freshly washed by the rain.

PRACTICAL GUIDE

1 Recovering in the sunshine are creamy violet scabious, spiky slate-blue echinops, the pinky-mauve crocus-like blooms of brodiaea, and the snowy pompons of camomile.

2 Pushed in together in happy disarray, they create an *ad hoc* posy of vulnerable charm.

3 Follow the same principle to rescue flowers from a larger bouquet that has wilted.

Sweet peas

Fragile as butterfly wings, sweet peas
have the shy grace of a half-wild
creature, briefly tamed. The implausibly
slender stems are leafless and barely
visible beneath the fluttering petals, the
filmy colors of which—palest yellows,
pastel pinks, ivory whites, delicate reds,
diaphanous purples—seem to capture
the essence of fresh, artless innocence.
As the flowers open, so their colors
grow ever paler and more translucent,
until finally this excess of elegance
expires in transparency. And as if all this
were not enough, sweet peas also have an
evocative perfume, hovering somewhere
between honey, roses, and lilac.

PRACTICAL GUIDE
1 While they add a touch of ethereal
lightness to mixed compositions,
nothing seems to suit sweet peas better
than being on their own.
2 In a simple arrangement such as this,
avoid adding foliage, as it tends to crush
and crumple the sweet pea petals.
3 For a simple arrangement, group the
sweet peas in bunches of a single color,
as on an old-fashioned florist's stall (see
following pages). If you wish to create a
more sophisticated bouquet, mingle the
different colors together.

*With their diaphanous colors
and delicately ruffled petals,
light and gauzy as silk,
sweet peas need no
accompaniment.*

Every summer, our house glows with bouquets of sweet peas, unrivaled in their freshness. Natural arrangements suit them best: here, a buttercup-yellow jug holds bunches of different colors, each more enchanting than the last. The narrow neck of the vase helps to support the slender stems.

Harmony in blue

If white and gold attract light into the house, blue seems to bring with it the peace of a tranquil, shady spot. Cool and haunting, blue is traditionally the color of immortality in China, while the West associates it with masculinity. It is daring to suggest creating a bouquet exclusively in blue, throwing the emphasis on the contrasts between different shades. Summer flowers, with their long stems, encourage expansive compositions such as this, so different from our customary posies.

Curiously, nature is rather stingy with blue flowers. Veronica, lupins, nigella, monkshood—these and a few others add up to barely a dozen species. Fall seems to have omitted blue almost entirely from its palette, but in summer—blue's favorite season—blue punctuates the garden, make refreshing pools of quietness for eyes weary of hotter colors.

Blue mixes well with white, yellow, orange, and some shades of green, which it makes more vibrant.

PRACTICAL GUIDE

1 In this arrangement, the slate blue of thistles, faded blue of agapanthus, and sky blue of delphiniums combine to create a dreamy blue cloud.

2 Oval-shaped vases with narrow necks are the most useful for free arrangements such as this, as they support the stems without the need for a flower-holder of any kind. The tall blue vase used here seems like a dark well of brightness in which the light is drowned.

3 When arranging the flowers in the vase, juxtapose the different species to ensure a balanced distribution of the various blues and a delicate play of shades and nuances.

4 Long flower spikes need more water than other blooms, so the vase will need frequent topping up.

5 This arrangement should stand close to a source of light, whether natural or artificial, so that its infinite variations on a theme are fully revealed.

Staked with care, delphiniums thrive in our Normandy garden, and their dreaming spires vivify sumptuous associations. Bathed in light, this bouquet of blue flowers reveals warmer notes of misty pink and mauve (below and opposite).

Fruits and flowers

After the harvest, fruits and flowers mingle in transparent bowls to create colorful and original table decorations.

Where fruit is concerned, there are good years and bad years, as anyone who is fortunate enough to have an orchard knows only too well. In good years, baskets brim with freshly picked cherries and apricots, while peaches and plums jostle for space, and the kitchen is transformed into a fragrant battlefield of simmering preserves and bubbling jams. Adults and children alike delight in this voluptuous cornucopia of ripe colors, textures, and scents which is the very essence of summer.

PRACTICAL GUIDE

1 What better way to celebrate this lavish abundance than by creating a fruit and flower arrangement? Plunge apricots, oranges, and lemons into a glass salad bowl filled with water.

2 Then use them to anchor violet lisianthus (also known as eustoma), softly speckled alstroemerias, slate-blue echinops, and "Ambiance" and "Sari" roses.

3 This summer pot-pourri will last for varying lengths of time according to the types of fruit used. Citrus fruits last better in water than more tender-skinned apricots and peaches. Lemons alone produce the longest-lasting effect with unclouded water.

4 The colors of the flowers are intense enough to hold their own against the glowing tones of the fruit. Blue flowers create the ultimate in contrasts.

5 For a delectable composition such as this to be successful, fruit and flowers must both appear to be drenched in the hot, pulsating sunlight of high summer.

Lunch al fresco

In summer, lunch becomes a tranquil pause in the shade of spreading trees. As the sun climbs to its zenith, glittering through the leafy boughs above, the garden spreads itself before your gaze like a still life; the warm air is laden with subtle perfumes, the leaves sparkle, and your only desire is to abandon yourself to this all-embracing stillness. Under the limes, a table is laid for Sunday lunch. The theme is simple blue and white, and the informal table decoration is inspired by the orchard close by.

PRACTICAL GUIDE

1 In this arrangement a cluster of peaches, looking as if they had just tumbled there, each holds a delicate, softly unfolding rose.

2 Ring the changes on the porcelain delicacy of the arrangement shown here with a sizzling combination of buttercup-yellow roses and golden lemons.

3 To maximize the effect of this simple celebration of nature's bounty, choose blooms that are well open.

4 Cut the stems of the roses short and on the diagonal. Then push the stems firmly into the top of the fruit. In these improvised vases, the roses drink the sweet juices of the fruit.

5 This is a partnership not destined to last much longer than the time it takes to eat lunch, but the subtlest and most successful table decorations are often the most ephemeral. Like the perfect guest, they know how to avoid outstaying their welcome, fading away discreetly as the festivities draw to a close.

Dappled sunlight filtering through tall trees, the scents and sounds of the still summer garden, and picnics in the green shade are childhood joys that still enliven adult spirits. Here, short-lived summer roses are plunged into a scattering of velvety peaches to create an al fresco *table decoration of childlike simplicity.*

Blues
and yellows

Sunny days are made for having fun with color. Here, a collection of pots and jugs that has brightened up the kitchen all winter is transported *en masse* to a shady corner of the garden, where it anchors a dazzling display of blues and yellows.

PRACTICAL GUIDE

1 The flowers in this type of arrangement may be of any shape or texture, provided their colors are of the required tonality and strength. Here, sunflowers, egg-yolk-yellow roses, and santolina serve as a counterpoint to the shimmering blue of cornflowers and the gauzy mauve of scabious—traditionally banned from the house as its filmy petals, which glow with such a strange light on stormy summer evenings, were thought to attract lightning. The three blues and three yellows form the perfect complement to each other, a combination of ravishing, nuance-free clarity.

2 This is a theme with many possible variations. Rich red dahlias, for example, would look stunning with the same yellows or with acid greens. Bear in mind simply that the flowers should always have the same unaffected directness as the rustic pots and jugs in which they are displayed.

3 Using a number of separate containers allows complete flexibility in playing with the heights and shapes of the different bouquets, the taller ones tending naturally to gravitate toward the back. Another advantage is that if the flowers in one container wilt before the others, they can be replaced with a fresh bouquet to restore sparkle to the whole ensemble.

4 This group of blues and yellows would be particularly at home in a sunny kitchen or dining room.

Enameled jugs and pots make unfussy containers for a collection of bouquets in forthright colors. This luminous composition exploits to the full the contrast between the intense blues of the scabious and cornflowers and the dazzling yellows of cornflowers, roses, and flowering santolina.

A flowered jug

Certain decorated vases lend themselves to lighthearted plays on the similarities between their floral motifs and the flowers they are chosen to hold. This green ceramic jug with its three white flowers in relief makes an irresistible combination with clusters of camomile and lacy wild carrot flowers. The spherical mounds of the carrot flowers are perfectly outlined by the waves of tiny camomile flowers, which seem to surge and froth around them. The white-and-green combination of the flowers, always irresistible, is here all the more enchanting for being reflected in the pattern of the jug.

PRACTICAL GUIDE

1 Matching containers with the arrangements that best reflect their decoration and coloring is an entertaining pastime for flower-lovers of all ages. By the same token, decorated vases do not bring out the best in bouquets which are very different in shape or coloring. A posy of small red and blue flowers, for instance, would look out of place in this jug.

2 For free, untied bouquets, choose a container with a narrow neck to emphasize the infectious sense of spontaneity.

3 Strip the camomile stalks, and cut them on the diagonal. Then gather together the flowers and insert them through the neck of the jug.

4 There is no need to include any foliage in this arrangement: its absence throws a greater emphasis on the contrast of textures between the two flowers.

5 Having decorated the table for a refreshing drink in the garden, this arrangement deserves a place in the lightest room in the house, where its soothing, refreshing qualities will be most evident.

A number of cultivated varieties of white carrot flower are now available. Perfect in combination with camomile flowers, they bring a touch of feathery lightness to any bouquet (left). With wild carrot flowers, camomile makes a composition of green-and-white freshness and spontaneity, echoed by the floral design of the narrow-necked ceramic jug (opposite).

Sunflowers

Exuberance is one of summer's prerogatives. Trees and shrubs, climbers and herbaceous plants all seem to rocket skyward—and how we yearn, secateurs in hand, to bring some of this profligacy of nature indoors! Sunflowers are one obvious way to do this. Larger than life, they grow to inordinate heights, turning their great daisy faces to the sun and lifting the spirits of all around.

The sturdy sunflower, flower of light, is magnificent on its own. Here we have preferred, nevertheless, to lighten the composition with trailing fronds of weeping willow and sculptural clouds of dill.

PRACTICAL GUIDE

1 The one drawback of sunflowers as cut flowers is the stiffness of their stems; they may, however, be softened by plunging them into a forest of greenery. Here, extravagant trails of weeping willow and clouds of dill, with its Japanese-looking yellow-green umbels, add volume and movement to the arrangement, while at the same time camouflaging the flower stalks.

2 For this arrangement we chose a zinc coal scuttle—both to provide a sturdy container and emphasize the informality of the flowers and the composition.

3 It is best to arrange compositions on this scale *in situ*. Once filled with water and flowers, containers such as this become almost impossible to move.

4 Prepare the willow branches in the same way as most foliage, crushing the ends with a hammer in order to help them take up water (see p. 141).

5 Cut the stems of the sunflowers and dill diagonally using secateurs. To create a stunning effect, cut the sunflowers slightly shorter than the surrounding foliage so that their half-submerged flowers shine out like beacons.

6 After this, place the fronds of foliage in the vase. They form the structure of the composition, the grey-green of the graceful willow leaves mingling prettily with the gold of the tiny dill flowers. Then insert the sunflowers into this elegant cloud of dull silver and gold.

Still life in zinc

We all have our passions—occasionally bordering on obsessions—and sometimes it is fun, in the clear light of summer, to take stock of the heights to which they have ascended. For this still life, we assembled an array of unrelated forms and objects with only one thing in common: zinc. Thus an eclectic medley of basins, milk churns, roof finials, Medici urns, boxes, acanthus wreaths, and more, found itself taking the air under the poplar trees one fine summer's day. Thrust into the open together, they immediately established a rapport which inspired us to arrange them according to size and shape, creating a kind of order out of chaos. The flowers followed quite naturally, as night follows day.

On one side, three varieties of thistle and a sheaf of lavender provided variations on the themes of blue-grey and grey-blue. On the other, the softly arching spires of a generous armful of purple buddleia awaited the clouds of butterflies that would surely not be long in coming.

PRACTICAL GUIDE

1 Zinc is equally at home inside the house as it is in the garden. Before using finds from markets and second-hand shops as vases, check them for holes. If you find any, line the containers with watertight objects or use synthetic foam, which is extremely easy to work with.
2 Cut the buddleia stems diagonally; partly strip them of their outer skin, and push them into blocks of pre-soaked synthetic foam. Simply plunge the thistles and lavender into water.

The slate-blues and grey-mauves of three varieties of thistle and a sheaf of lavender marry perfectly with the powdery pewter greys of zinc urns, troughs, and buckets (below).

Our collection of zinc utensils grows larger with every passing year. We regularly fill our new acquisitions with flowers: here, a lavish armful of buddleia, with its intoxicating spicy perfume, graces a zinc urn (left).

Dried globes

The spherical flowerheads of eryngium retain their subtle dove-grey shades as they dry, while statice remains faithful to its delicate blush-pink (below).

Even if—as the evenings begin to lengthen imperceptibly and the heat of the sun starts to wane—nature seems to redouble its efforts to convince us that summer will go on for ever, sooner or later we have reluctantly to admit that it won't. Now is the time to make that effort of the imagination, to think ahead to the dark days of winter, when the barely faded colors of dried flowers seem patiently to await the return of spring.

Prepared as summer draws to a close, spheres of dried flowers will retain their charm for many months to come. Sulphur-yellow achillea, faded cinnamon scabious, pink or gold statice, echinops, thistles, lavender, poppy seedheads, and grasses lend themselves to an infinite number of associations (opposite).

Dried flowers are not eternal, however, and it is salutary to replace those dusty, cobweb-laden bouquets of summers past with fresher, more colorful offerings.

PRACTICAL GUIDE

1 Florists' shops and garden centers now stock spherical balls of synthetic foam. Studding these with fresh flowers for drying is child's play.

2 For obvious reasons of balance, it is important to choose the size of the flowers to suit the size of the ball. The slate-blue heads of echinops, still-green poppy seedheads, and the intriguing segmented seedheads of scabious, all three globe-shaped themselves, are best suited to smaller balls. Achillea, statice, and lavender work better on larger ones.

3 Whatever size of ball you are using, it is a wise precaution to start by tying a length of string round it, so that you will be able to hang it up to dry without crushing the flowers or seedheads.

4 In all cases, cut the flower stems as short as possible, retaining only the part that is to be pushed into the foam.

5 Push flowers in until the globe is completely covered. You may make globes of a single color, or, for a softer effect, mix different species.

6 Hang the finished globes in a warm, dry, dark place for a few weeks to become glowing still lives, perfect for brightening the gloom of winter. They may be displayed equally well in isolation or arranged in groups.

Fall

Green in bud, flushing crimson in flower, sweet scabious (Scabiosa atropurpurea) shares the rich, earthy colors of fall, just as its lavender-blue cousin, S. caucasica, seems to to mirror the summer sky (above).

Clusters of dull gold viburnum berries, deep red amaranthus plumes, glossy chestnut hypericum berries, coppery roses, and the yellow coxcombs of celosias combine in a fall bouquet which appeals to our passion for profusion and excess (opposite).

The honey-colored light of a September morning heralds the poignant decline of summer into fall. The sun, now tinged with russet, hangs lower in the sky, and the plump, tawny apples are poised to fall. Usurper of the languorous days of summer and harbinger of winter's bleak chill, fall has the most unenviable role of all the seasons. And yet, this is the moment when the chrysanthemums, large and small, erupt in all shades of rich bronze and flame colors, defying us to subside into a mood of wistful nostalgia. Not to be outdone, the dahlias—from tiny pompons to blowsy exhibition blooms—raise their flamboyant heads above the disheveled remains of the summer borders, smoldering like hot coals in the fall mists, as though to dazzle us into forgetting their lack of perfume. The asters, meanwhile, make a more discreet entrance, combining their yellow centers and luminescent lavender-mauve petals with faultless color sense, or flooding the borders with rivers of hot carmine pink. Add to these the outrageous spikes of gladioli, the glowing tassels of amaranthus, satin-petaled lisianthus, and celosias with their astonishing scarlet velvet coxcombs, and you begin to feel the warmth and vibrancy of nature's last glorious flourish before the onset of winter.

up for this in intensity. And while the tall spires of some summer blooms inspire spreading arrangements, fall's dense clusters of glowing color seem to fall naturally into round posies punctuated by foliage.

In the face of brisk winds and lowering skies, windows are firmly closed, curtains are drawn, and fires lit. After two seasons of open doors, limpid light, and translucent materials, the emphasis is now on solidity and texture. If spring is visual, fall is tactile. Now is the time to put away those glass vases, and dust off heavy earthenware jugs, stoneware pots, and metal troughs. Less self-effacing and more assertive than the fragile containers of spring and summer, they actively complement the bouquets they hold, setting off the sultry colors of the flowers with their own more somber tones.

In this season of transition, the house becomes a place of warm welcome, ushering in the dazzling colors, aromatic perfumes, and luscious fruit that only fall can yield. To do justice to these gifts, all we have to do is match fall's generosity with a similar sense of luxuriant abundance.

Yet fall has other cards up her sleeve, for this is the season when foliage comes into its own. Purple-red American white oak, variegated dogwood, dusky raspberry leaves, and violet-flushed peppermint are only some of the rich variety now available. In their kaleidoscopic array of earthy, warm colors and their sensual textures, fall leaves are far more than mere padding, lending an extra dimension to fall bouquets. This season of harvest and plenty also provides a rich crop of fruits and berries, soul mates of both foliage and flowers, with which they form artfully subtle or dramatic partnerships.

While fall's palette may be more restricted than that of summer, with blue virtually absent, it more than makes

Massing bunches of different flowers within a bouquet is an effective means of exploiting contrasts of color and texture to the full. "Sari" roses, just beginning to unfold, blowsy dahlias, speckled alstroemerias, and carthamus here combine in an incandescent display of blazing color (above).

Cactus and decorative dahlias in a range of fiery tones from fuchsia pink to flaming red and sizzling orange put on a firework display which dazzles us into forgetting their lack of perfume (opposite).

The season of harvests and fruit-picking, fall is the time for ingenious arrangements featuring fruits and berries, hips and haws, playing on their plentiful variety of contrasting colors, shapes, and textures. Berries now festoon many flowering shrubs, their glossy colors favoring spectacular compositions, and the hedgerows are full of equally eye-catching wild rosehips. With its contrasting reds and greens, and matt and shiny surfaces, and its vivid contrast between the nuts with their ferocious defences and the berries with their provocative splendor designed to entice the birds, this bouquet captures the changing moods of fall.

PRACTICAL GUIDE

1 In this shallow bowl, clusters of pink-flushed "Everest" crab apples rub

shoulders with the shiny, tomato-red hips of a rugosa rose among reddish-purple American white oak leaves, while sweet chestnut cases, prickly as sea urchins, form a dramatic contrast with the liquid scarlet of ripe viburnum berries.

2 As crab apples bear clusters of fruit along the length of their branches, it is possible to economize by cutting them into sections of equal length. Used in this way, two branches were sufficient for this composition.

3 First line the shallow wooden bowl with an impermeable layer of cellophane or aluminum foil. Then place a pre-soaked block of synthetic foam in it.

4 As this low composition is intended to be viewed from above, it is important to ensure that the foam is well hidden. Cut all branches short, arranging them densely, and revolving the bowl so that you work from all sides.

5 Start by inserting a forest of oak leaves into the foam, taking care to reserve the largest leaves for the outer edges.

6 After this, add the short branches laden with berries and fruits, making them appear to nestle quite naturally among the leaves, alternating colors, shapes, and textures to achieve the best visual effect.

7 This arrangement would look splendid in the center of an unlaid dining room table, or—better still—on a low table.

A lack of flowers does not have to imply a lack of color. A shallow bowl is filled with a luminous composition of berries, leaves, and fruit in a

satisfying variety of textures. In its dense and colorful profusion, it seems to symbolize the aesthetic richness and prodigal abundance of the harvest season (above, left, and opposite).

Fall pastels

When fall is not in a mood for brilliant scarlets and oranges, it suffuses gardens and the countryside with a misty veil of muted pastel shades. Inspired by their mellow softness, this bouquet brings together flowers and foliage in delicate tones, not massing them in bunches but rather dotting single stems about, so that the different species and colors mingle together in a pastel-tinted haze.

Like a flower border veiled in the first October mists, this posy combining the pastel tones of roses and dahlias with different greens of carefully chosen foliage possesses a lingering, dreamlike charm.

PRACTICAL GUIDE

1 Creamy "Cafe au Lait" dahlias seem a world apart from the brassy boldness that we normally associate with this flower. The delicate nuances of their tones are picked up by the yellow of neat "Barok" roses and the lilac-pink crumpled blooms of *R.* "Mamy Blue." Washed-out hydrangeas, the trailing tassels of "Queue-de-Renard" amaranthus, plumes of pennisetum, and a few branches of raspberry leaves contribute as many different tones of green, sometimes shading to yellow. Volume is added by the more discreet deep green foliage of mahonia, prettily edged in red, and box.

2 Choose a vase to echo the shape of the posy and accentuate the impression of lavish abundance; the bronze vase we chose works well.

3 Carefully separate the stems, and strip them of their lower leaves.

4 Then arrange them in a large posy (see p. 143), alternating flowers and foliage to ensure a harmonious combination of colors and textures. In this composition, establishing the right balance is of prime importance, so mix the different species thoroughly so that no single type predominates.

5 When trailing flowers form part of a bouquet, always arrange them around the rim of the vase. Here, the softly arching plumes of "Queue-de-Renard" amaranthus add a note of lightness and grace to the composition.

6 This posy is designed to be viewed from above, so place it on a low table close to a source of light, which will reveal the soft shadings of its misty colors.

Of cabbages and dahlias...

When you have only a bunch or two of flowers to fill a large container, foliage provides the perfect solution. Here a few "Mercedes Rubirosa" dahlias, which delight us every year with their creamy pink camellia-shaped blooms and rich softness, make a delightful composition with a couple of pink-centered, prettily variegated ornamental cabbages against a leafy background of surprising depth and textural interest. Purple-flushed eucalyptus, crocosmia seedheads on their arching sprays, a bough of dark green viburnum, and the airy foliage of mimosa make a gracefully sculptural setting for the dahlia blooms (see following pages).

PRACTICAL GUIDE

1 The flowers are sturdy and imposing, and yet, thanks to the pastel shades of the dahlias, cabbages, and some of the foliage, the arrangement does not give the slightest impression of heaviness.
2 We chose to display this arrangement in a weighty jardiniere which we found in Normandy. It balances the voluminous composition, as well as providing a sturdy base.

3 It is advisable to create a large arrangement such as this *in situ* in order to avoid having to move it. This has the added advantage of enabling you to place the foliage according to the setting.
4 Arrange the foliage in a nonchalant, careless fashion, leaving it in sheaves to give the impression of a barrowful of prunings, tossed in pellmell. The sheaves of foliage establish their own sense of balance among themselves, and the points where their stems cross make ideal flower-holders for dahlias and cabbages.
5 Group the cabbages and dahlias toward the center in order to highlight their pretty salmon pinks. Had they been dotted about at random among the foliage, the eye would not have been drawn to the flowers, but rather to the empty spaces between them.
6 The flowers will fade before the foliage, but they can easily be replaced with a fresh handful of blooms of the same color, thus restoring the *éclat* of the whole arrangement.
7 This spreading composition needs to be raised up so as not to get in the way: a pedestal would show it off perfectly.

The softly rounded petals of these decorative dahlias evoke the exquisite winter blooms of camellias, not only in form but also in texture.

Dahlias are as easy to cultivate as they are spectacular to look at. In Normandy, they have their own corner of our potager, so that we can pick them to make arrangements for the house each weekend in fall. Nestling among a graceful display of foliage, these decorative dahlias, together with a couple of ornamental cabbages in the same tones, impart a sense of careless abundance to the whole composition.

Luxuriant chrysanthemums

Faced with a narrow-necked container, our first instinct is to reach for long-stemmed flowers—but this is not always the most interesting solution. This imposing crackle-glazed earthenware vase inspired an unusual approach based on the low, spreading shape of a bouquet of chrysanthemums and dogwood.

PRACTICAL GUIDE

1 We chose the densely creamy chrysanthemum "Avignon Blanc" for its subtle harmonies with the vase. The carmine-flushed foliage of a variegated dogwood made a flattering companion, and the sumptuous pink chrysanthemums we happened to find at our supplier's that day proved a miraculously perfect match with both. These large chrysanthemums, grown under glass, are the fruit of long years of research involving the most frothily voluminous blooms available.

2 When exceptional blooms such as these are not available, we often use "Tom Pearce" chrysanthemums and strong russet foliage. The handsome, round flowers of this variety come in particularly flamboyant tones, shading from deep orange to the browns and burnt umber of fall undergrowth, with touches of red on some petals.

3 It is impossible to use flower-holders in narrow-necked vases. Start the arrangement with the foliage stems to enable the flowers to find the necessary support at the points where they intersect.

4 Arrange the dogwood branches first, with the stems sloping inside the vase to reduce the height of the foliage as far as possible. The resulting tousled cushion of twisting, pastel-toned foliage, recalls the soft light of certain fall days.

5 Then position the chrysanthemum blooms, pushing them in far enough to nestle delicately among the leaves—an approach which has the double advantage of masking the not particularly attractive stems of the flowers while enhancing the lightness of the dogwood.

6 Check the water level every other day, as chrysanthemums and foliage both drink a lot.

7 This elegant arrangement would be well suited to a library or hallway.

Less commonly found than orange or bronze varieties, these cream and pink chrysanthemums are combined with variegated dogwood foliage which echoes their tones faithfully. The low, spreading bouquet is held in an unusual crackle-glazed earthenware vase, whose round shape would be equally well suited to a tall arrangement (left and opposite).

Dahlias
of distinction

Some blooms are as exquisite as collector's items. And if the splendor of these rare two-tone decorative dahlias is only fleeting, then so be it: the pleasure we take in contemplating them is all the greater for being so precarious (opposite).

A chance encounter with a flower of exceptional quality may stop you in your tracks. Occasionally, as we wander down the aisles of the flower market at Rungis, our eye is caught by some particular species or other which immediately stands out by virtue of its color or texture.

The haste with which we rush to buy the few available bunches of the rare bloom is tinged with the excitement a collector must feel when fate brings him face to face with a unique and priceless piece. On the day in question, a clutch of two-tone decorative dahlias with all the splendor of Chinese lacquer lit up the gloom of a grey October dawn and instantly enslaved us. Even when buying flowers is part of your working day, encounters of this nature give rise to a sense of indescribable delight. Having wrapped up our find with infinite care, we bore it home with us as though it were a precious treasure. Without a word being spoken, we both knew—in the first transports of this jealous passion—that the object of our devotion would not be joining the other flowers in the shop. We chose a smooth, glistening, midnight-blue earthenware pot as the receptacle worthy of receiving our dahlias. So spectacular that they did not need to be mixed with any other flowers or foliage, once in their vase they immediately unleashed a thousand blazing points of fire, which danced on the walls of the modern workshop in which they stood and from which we could not tear our eyes away.

PRACTICAL GUIDE

1 Another small dahlia, "Caporal," is almost equally luminous, with brilliant red flowers above lovely dark foliage. This also deserves to be displayed on its own.

2 The gleaming curves of glazed terracotta set off the exuberance of dahlias to perfection.

3 The blooms of decorative dahlias such as this are held at right angles to their stems. In order to avoid having all the flowers facing in the same direction, leave a gap in the center of the vase, and place them back to back.

4 Dahlias' reputation for having a short life in water is richly deserved. The longest-lasting dahlias are pompon varieties. In all cases, add a few drops of bleach diluted in the water to extend their lives.

A marriage of opposites: purple and orange

Some color combinations belong exclusively to fall. The massed arrangement of this flamboyant bouquet exploits to the full the moody depth of the purple asters and the glowing orange of the cactus-flowered dahlias (below and opposite).

Before the dark days of winter finally set in, the flowers of fall seem to enjoy one last glorious fling, decking themselves out in the most vibrant colors of the spectrum. This bouquet, so typical of the season, combines shades almost never seen in the garden at other times of year.

PRACTICAL GUIDE

1 In this composition, for example, only the dense purple of robust "Boy" asters would do to set off the blazing intensity of these cactus-flowered dahlias. The hypericum used to provide foliage offers the bonus of flowers and berries of childlike charm.

2 When arranging vibrant flowers, choose a vase in neutral colors, such as this eggshell buff one, which makes no attempt to compete with the flamboyant colors of the flowers.

3 Hypericum, with its dense branches and sturdy flowers, provides the skeleton of the arrangement. Put this in place first.

4 Make the most of saturated colors by massing each species in bunches of five or six stems (see p. 143), thus setting off a firework display of searing contrasts. This is a method very much in vogue at the moment, but it is no mere fad: not only does it exploit colors to the full, it also enables smaller flowers to hold their own against larger ones. This combination of asters and giant dahlias demonstrates the point perfectly: dotted about, the asters would undoubtedly have been overwhelmed; used *en masse*, they create pools of luminous purple against the orange.

5 A dark background makes a perfect foil for arrangements such as this, which also need space around them so that they can be admired from a little distance.

Crimson scabious

Some flowers are so familiar in particular shades that we may completely forget that they exist in other colors as well. Scabious, for instance, is virtually synonymous with filmy lavender-blues and mauves. We may have come across greeny-white or sugar-pink varieties, but the crimson scabious is so seldom found that on first encountering it we might be tempted to mistake it for a miniature sweet william. In recent years, a handful of small growers have attempted to relaunch this spectacular variety, whose palette ranges from maroon to magenta, via every shade of crimson and claret. Indeed, if blue scabious is the flower of summer, red is the creature of fall, mingling its wine-dark petals with the rich, earthy colors of berries and fallen leaves.

For us, the search for unusual flowers and rare colors is part of the florist's art. When we have the opportunity to do so, it gives us genuine pleasure to share our "finds" with our clientele, and we can never emphasize enough the affection and respect that we feel for the few devoted growers who overcome innumerable obstacles in their quest to re-establish long-neglected varieties.

PRACTICAL GUIDE

1 The idea of combining two species of flower with the same glowing, wine-dark tones is open to a huge number of variations. The crimson-red tassels of "Pendula" amaranthus add a note of velvety voluptuousness, while vying with the scabious in the richness of their coloring. Choose foliage that is neither too heavy nor too dense, so that it does not steal the flowers' thunder.
2 Black containers—here a painted metal trough—are particularly effective with predominantly red bouquets.
3 Start by making a chicken wire mesh to provide support for the flowers and foliage (see p. 142).
4 Then arrange the bush of peppermint foliage, flushed purple by the chill of fall, followed by the flowers. Position the amaranthus so that it hangs down over the edges of the container.
5 With its rich coloring and velvety textures, this arrangement would suit a room decorated in somber tones—perhaps a snugly upholstered, book-lined study.

Better known in shades of lavender and blue, scabious has the sturdy grace of a true old-fashioned garden flower. The crimson variety, or sweet scabious, ranges in color from maroon and purple to cherry red and

Scabious are displayed to best advantage in compact arrangements, such as this one including peppermint foliage. The trailing tassels of amaranthus echo the crimsons and magentas of the scabious while adding a touch of feathery lightness to the composition (opposite).

magenta, the tiny florets opening out to reveal plump pincushions of snowy white styles (below).

Although we love gladioli, we cannot say that we have received much encouragement to do so. A flower that is still all too often relegated to the foyers of grand hotels, it has considerable virtues, and its rehabilitation is long overdue. True, it has received a bad press, and the current taste for posies tends to leaves its long spikes sticking out like a sore thumb. But for high-rise arrangements in tall vases, nothing can rival the stately grandeur of a sheaf of gladioli.

Cut gladioli are tough and extremely long-lasting, but these virtues are as nothing beside the breathtaking range of their colors, from velvety pinks and peachy yellows, through mauves and purples, to whites of startling purity. They are also reasonably priced and easy

to find, although some florists tend to stock them only in red.

PRACTICAL GUIDE

1 To look their best, gladioli need to be massed together in generous numbers. Choose several bunches in different colors. To temper their stiffness, we like to surround them with a ruff of foliage or grasses. Here we chose the downy quills of *Miscanthus sinensis* to add a sense of movement and lightness. As well as camouflaging the rigid gladioli stems, a bushy nimbus such as this also adds volume to this colorful, upwardly mobile arrangement.

2 Owing to their height gladioli require a relatively heavy container. We chose a glass vase decorated with a filigree of dull metal wire.

3 To ensure that the flowers open fully along the length of the stems, remove the topmost four or five buds from each spike. This is the only precaution necessary to ensure a dramatic display.

4 Insert the gladioli in the vase, balancing their stems around the inside of the container to make it stable.

5 This display should last at least a week.

In a bulbous-based glass vase encased in wire filigree, gladioli make a stately and dramatic display, exploiting the rich depth of their velvety colors. A ruff of light and supple grasses adds a horizontal dimension to an otherwise vertical composition (above, left, and opposite).

One vase,
three bouquets

*I*dentical vases often come in different sizes, although these do not necessarily suit matching bouquets. These three nesting vases, grouped together on a pretty mahogany table, hold three classically autumnal bouquets which contrive to complement each other without allowing any one to dominate the others.

GLADIOLI AND FOLIAGE

The tallest of the three bouquets is all volume and movement, with disparate masses of pale yellow gladioli and boughs of American white oak. The foliage forms the backdrop to the composition, while the sheaf of gladioli seems to sink back into it, its spikes cutting across the rounded mass of oak leaves and lending direction to the branches. The pastel shade of the blooms was chosen to soften some of the red tones of the foliage.

COPPER AND CERISE

In front of this voluminous composition is a posy (see p.143) playing on contrasts of copper and cerise. Hot orange marigolds, dashing fuchsia-pink celosias, sedate dusty pink "Leonidas" roses, and a large tawny chrysanthemum create bold associations in a rich, glowing palette, punctuated by the watered silk of the eucalyptus-like foliage of *Protea cordata*.

SINGLE DAHLIA

The third, goblet-sized vase holds a single decorative dahlia bloom, the roundness of its softly incurved flame-colored petals echoed by the *Protea cordata* leaves against which it sits. The balance between the flower and the foliage in this pared-down bouquet reproduces in microcosm the equilibrium of the composition as a whole.

PRACTICAL GUIDE

1 When grouping together three vases to create a single effect, link them by the colors of the flowers you are using.
2 The success of this autumn trilogy depends on the complementary nature of the colors making up the three bouquets: the merest touch of white or blue would be enough to upset the fine balance of smouldering earth colors.
3 When using a single much larger bloom (here the chrysanthemum) as part of a bouquet, always position it to one side. Placed centrally it would appear too dominant, overwhelming the other flowers.

Three versions of the same vase in different sizes can be used to hold bouquets of quite disparate shapes and sizes. The flowers chosen here, arranged alone, in a neat posy, or completely naturally, share a range of smoldering fall tones. The success of the composition as a whole is assured by the close rapport between the three bouquets (opposite).

Velvet and silk: lisianthus and celosias

*A*nyone who enjoys continually putting their creativity to the test should never hold back from the temptation to try out adventurous combinations of flowers. Playing with unexpected or surprising contrasts of color and texture always gives us tremendous pleasure—as the bouquet shown here demonstrates. Light and soft as silk scarves, lisianthus (also known as eustoma) are a relatively recent introduction which appeared in florists' shops only a few years ago.

Fill conical vases with water before adding the flowers, otherwise there is always a danger that the weight of flower stems pressing against the rim will tip them over (below).

Although the name is unfamiliar to many people, few will forget its looks, and particularly its unusual, softly spiralled buds. Long and graceful and held on slender, sinuous stems, the buds gradually unfold to reveal flowers of startling beauty, with glossy, delicately curved petals in a seductive palette of subtlest blues, whites, and pinks. With its clear, elegant lines and its enchanting range of colors, the lisianthus has—not surprisingly—become extremely popular.

PRACTICAL GUIDE

1 The satiny purples of the lisianthus make a bold contrast with the densely crumpled chiffons and velvets of the crimson celosias, with a small cluster of amaranthus holding aloft their more discreet rose-pink plumes beside them.
2 Avoid buying celosias with heads that are too big, as the stems are not strong enough to support them without snapping.
3 Trim the stems with a knife or secateurs, and arrange the flowers freely, not attempting to impose any particular structure on them. Ensure that the different species are closely intermingled, so as to create the most vivid contrasts between them. Position the shortest stems at the front of the bouquet, an essential technique with vases of this shape to ensure volume and depth.
4 With its striking effects of color and texture, this unusual bouquet would look sensational in an uncluttered modern interior.

The exhilarating freedom with which the colors of the celosias and lisianthus are associated ensures the dramatic effect of this arrangement, which would look extremely striking in a modern, rather masculine setting in warm dark tones (opposite).

November
tea party

*Small pompon
chrysanthemums are known
as fall daisies by the
Chinese. Once the long,
gangly stems have been cut*

*down, the luminous and
compact blooms make classic
posies of perfect proportions
(above).*

In France, chrysanthemums suffer from rather morbid associations, for this is the flower that tranforms every cemetery into a spectacular floral display on All Saints' Day each year. Clients who might otherwise be tempted by cheerful little pompons or sprays turn away at the mere mention of the name. In the face of such injustice, we have no choice but to cheat. The Chinese call chrysanthemums fall daisies—and so (now) do we.

Although these three posies vary in the choice of plants used, the technique used for all of them is the same.

PRACTICAL GUIDE

1 Unlike some flowers, the little chrysanthemums used here are not displayed to best advantage on their own. It is almost always preferable to mix them with berries or foliage: here the deep chestnut berries of hypericum, the pink berries of cotoneaster, and the fall-tinted leaves of Virginia creeper, chosen because their glossy texture sets off the warm tones of the blooms and the berries.

2 Nothing seems to suit small chrysanthemums better than a posy, an arrangement to which they invariably contrive—as can be seen from these examples—to contribute an infallible sense of proportion.

3 First of all, strip the chrysanthemum stems of leaves, and trim them to the desired length. Chrysanthemums owe their stiffness to their long, ungainly stems, which distract from the pretty pompons of the flowers. In cutting the stems right down, we always feel we are improving on nature by bestowing on the blooms the proportions they deserve.

4 Then cut the stems of the berries to the same length as the chrysanthemums.

5 Make a posy (see p. 143), alternating between the chrysanthemum stems and the berries.

6 Tie the posy, and encircle it with five or six purple-green Virginia creeper leaves. Then tie the whole composition together firmly. Tying both before and after the Virginia creeper leaves ensures that the stems are securely fixed and will not slip.

7 Placed in amber-tinted glasses to decorate a November tea table, these posies will happily last for at least a week.

8 They look charming on any small stand or coffee table, their coppery tones marrying well with warm materials, especially polished wood.

*With their colors of bright
fire and setting sun,
chrysanthemums look best
positioned against wood,
which reflects the warm
glints of the flowers
(opposite).*

Fruits of the season

Fruit and flowers together create palatable associations of exhilarating color and tempting curves. With their appealing looks and evocative perfume, dessert apples—speared on sticks like toffee apples—make an unusual and inimitable seasonal display.

Apples are to fall as tulips are to spring. They punctuate the leaves now littering lawns and orchard floors, and fill the house with their delicious ripe scent. In partnership with flowers, apples also reveal a highly decorative side to their irrepressibly cheerful character, making bouquets that look quite literally good enough to eat.

PRACTICAL GUIDE

1 It is easy to create such an unexpected arrangement of flowers, foliage, and fruit. Here we chose flowers in the exhilarating oranges of fall: peppery-scented, round-faced marigolds, velvety "Ambiance" roses, and flame-colored montbretia, like slender tongues of fire. For the foliage we used the handsome, deeply cut leaves of liquidambar from our garden, but maple leaves, which are very similar, would produce the same colorful effect. The somber berries of the hypericum need to be balanced by a further splash of color, here provided by scarlet-berried cotoneaster, its more exuberant lookalike. The crowning glory are the crisp, tawny apples, held aloft on sticks like toffee apples from the fairs of our childhood. Glossy mahogany-brown sweet chestnuts, grouped in clusters of three or four, would make an equally effective substitute for the apples.

2 Choose a robust, wide-necked vase or bowl, such as this square vase in a blend of terracottas. With its rustic charm it reminded us of the warm, dark, sweet-smelling barns in Normandy where apples are stored for the winter.

3 First, put some crumpled chicken wire in the bottom of the vase to act as a flower-holder.

4 When you are satisfied with the shape of the chicken wire, start by positioning the foliage that forms the bouquet's basic structure. After this add the berries and the flowers.

5 Last of all prepare the apples on sticks. The sticks used are small canes bought from a garden center, cut diagonally at one end with secateurs. Push one end of the stick into the apple, ensuring that the apple is secure, then poke the other end of the stick through the chicken wire. Placing the apples is like having fun with a construction kit. In order to create the right sense of volume and density, you need to take care to display them from all sides and at different heights within the arrangement.

6 Displayed on a small table in a place where its perfumes and colors can be enjoyed to the full, this little bouquet will bring all the pleasures of fall into your living room.

Gourds
and squashes

Smooth or warty, striped or speckled, tall or squat, pistachio green or lemon yellow, biscuit beige or marmelade orange—gourds and squashes celebrate harvest time in their own eccentric fashion and with tremendous *brio*.
In our childhood, when the sight of an idle child produced an almost allergic reaction, November was the month when these curious vegetables were pressed into small hands by adults proffering tips on how to turn them into possibly even more curious objects. Old habits die hard: children can make these quirky vases or candle-holders with the minimum of adult intervention.

PRACTICAL GUIDE

1 Here, a purple-blue hydrangea bloom and gauzy lavender nigella look quite at home in their unconventional improvised vases, while a beautiful creamy-apricot butternut squash flatters the mauves and oranges of a nosegay of irises (see following pages).

2 An assortment of foliage studded with a few berries would make an attractive substitute for flowers in these unusual arrangements. Try, for instance, the laurel-like leaves of *Viburnum tinus* with trails of dark green ivy and orange cotoneaster or pyracantha berries.

3 Start by drawing a line round the gourd or squash to show where the top should be cut off. Adults can then help by cutting the tops off with a sharp knife and hollowing out the pulp with an ice-cream scoop, taking care not to pierce the skin of those intended as vases.

4 Cut the stems of all the flowers as short as possible so that when you place them in the "vase" they camouflage the cut mark.

5 Make posies, following the advice on page 143.

6 For the candle-holder, place a delicate little cushion of lichen, its coloring in shades of verdigris marrying perfectly with the different greens of the gourds, around the lip of the gourd, to disguise the cut.

7 These weird and wonderful creations would make a cheerful and amusing decoration massed together on a hearth or window-sill.

Gourds and squashes—in all their astonishing variety—make unusual and amusing vases. Here they hold clutches of iris and nigella with their stems cut very short.

Warty and knobbly as wicked witches' chins, or improbably smooth and voluptuously creamy, gourds and squashes all belong to the vast and genially eccentric family of Cucurbitaceae, which also includes marrows and pumpkins. Adults and children alike can have fun making delightfully quirky vases and candle-holders such as these.

Pumpkins
and peppers

*I*s it possible to tire of flowers? One day, a client burst into the shop, declaring loudly that she wanted a spectacular buffet decoration, but one without any flowers. "I'm bored with flowers," she protested. "Find me something different!" And thus this vegetable bouquet was born. It is not often that florists have a gauntlet such as this flung down before them, and we accepted the challenge.

It was fall. Whatever brainwave we were to come up with had to respect the colors of the season. Orange. Orange as the beaks of the blackbirds hopping across our lawn. Orange as a leaf-strewn woodland path under a burnished October sun. Orange as a pumpkin! The pumpkins in our kitchen garden were perfectly plump, waxy smooth, and truly, divinely orange against the bare blackness of the November soil. We had found our vase!

A majestic pumpkin—plump, gleaming, and resplendently orange—makes a grandiose foil for a piquant display of chilli peppers and ornamental cabbages in similarly pungent colors. A hollowed-out pumpkin makes an impressive and oddly versatile vase (opposite).

PRACTICAL GUIDE

1 With studious care we sliced off the bottom of the pumpkin, hollowing out the pulp with a heavy spoon like an ice-cream scoop (and keeping it to make a delicious soup, *naturellement*). All we had to do now was fill it with water and find something to put in it.

2 Nothing should be allowed to deaden the impact of that magnificent flaming orange. On the other hand, few colors would be able to hold their own in the face of such shameless competition. The choice was not easy. Some handsome mauve ornamental cabbages provided the answer to our dilemma, their rich coloring accentuating the flamboyant orange of the pumpkin without sacrificing any of its own intensity.

3 Trusses of orange and yellow chilli peppers were the obvious next step. A third color would have introduced unnecessary confusion and blunted the power of the composition. Pointed like pixie hats, the chilli peppers provided an amusing transition between the cabbages and their singular container, while at the same time matching the heroically squat and heavy pumpkin with their lightness.

4 We arranged the cabbages in clusters of two or three, filling the gaps with the labyrinthine branches of the chilli peppers. The stems of the cabbages and chilli peppers have sufficient weight and thickness to support themselves without the need for a flower-holder.

5 If a different solution with more flexible and fragile stems is chosen (such as a bouquet of wild rosehips), fill the pumpkin with pre-soaked synthetic foam, and insert the stems one by one.

6 A hollowed-out pumpkin lends itself to all sorts of different arrangements. Fall foliage and fruits (apples, chestnuts etc., speared on short canes) would look particularly fine displayed in this manner.

Winter

Headily fragrant and elegantly showy, lilies can be relied upon to brighten the dark winter months with the opalescent whiteness of their graceful petals (above).

The Christmas rose or hellebore is rash enough to flower in the garden in the depths of December. Here, the creamy opaqueness of its ivory petals is set off by a French East India Company porcelain vase, while their magenta flush is echoed by the spiky, purple-green leaves of mahonia (opposite).

Bare trees and desolate black earth under a sullen sky of lead are the inescapable hallmarks of winter. Serenely awaiting the return of spring, the house now becomes inward-looking, a haven of snug comfort in which flowers and foliage are doubly welcome. The fireside is the focus of life, and few pleasures can vie with the luxury of sinking into a deep armchair beside a crackling log fire. Accordingly, winter bouquets are to be found on low tables in the warmest, cosiest spots, where they can most conveniently be admired.

Raw materials now being scarce, imagination and flair must make up the shortfall. Rare though they may be, the flowers of winter offer generous size and voluptuousness, richly aromatic scents and colors of fathomless depths. Now more than ever, they deserve a place of honor in the house. Plump and round as a cat curled up in front of the fire, winter bouquets mingle the reds, blues, and whites of flowers with the greys and deep greens of evergreen foliage, now an invaluable source of sculptural textures and gleaming colors to brighten the long, dark days. Ferociously prickly holly, pretty purple-green mahonia, ivy, box, and yew are some of the mainstays of winter, alongside the brilliant berries and fruits that bring memories of fall's lavish abundance.

Flowers now available include fragile anemones and ranunculus, orchids as exquisite as jewels, spectacular and stately amaryllis, chastely pure hellebores, and intoxicatingly fragrant tuberoses. Together with hothouse pinks and carnations, lilies, roses, and tulips, they lend themselves with equal success to virtuoso displays of shimmering color and—at the opposite end of the spectrum—to delicately transparent compositions with all the glittering, ethereal translucency of hoar frost. Exotic varieties imported from South Africa also now become available, making an invaluable contribution to Christmas decorations with their rugged hardiness and rich color range.

As the garden sleeps, vases shrug off the self-effacing rustic simplicity of summer to emerge as stylish objets in their own right. Porcelain, colored glass, and silver encourage compositions of consummate elegance, framing carefully chosen flowers as though they were valuable ornaments. But their reign is not unchallenged: favorite spring and summer vases may well reappear in the depths of winter, trimmed with a ruff of dried flowers to freshen their looks or shield their transparency.

With the approach of Christmas, finally, the house is transformed: in a flurry of activity and excitement, it is decked with garlands and wreaths, and filled with aromatic scents and flickering candlelight. The Christmases we love most—whether traditionally red and green or elegantly white as snow—are those that bear an unmistakably personal stamp. Some of our own designs for Christmas are included here with pleasure, in the hope that they may kindle in others the childlike delight which is so much a part of Christmas—and that they may testify to our own cherished belief that there is no precious moment so happy, no special day so festive, as one that is celebrated with flowers.

Orchids are the silky and exotic butterflies of winter, trapping the pale winter light in their sensual, fleshy petals. In a fine, white porcelain vase, two different varieties glow in a captivating range of pinks and mauves (above).

Heathery statice, downy dove-grey kochis, eucalyptus seedpods and the spheres of silverbrunia combine to produce a subtle and long-lasting play of color and texture, with pools of gleaming light provided by white ranunculus (opposite).

Simple anemones

Very occasionally, an apparently trivial incident can have life-changing repercussions. In our case, our decision to open Mille Feuilles was born of a fruitless quest for blue anemones. We had been invited to dinner by a friend who adored blue anemones, and a huge bunch of them, we thought, would make a perfect gift. But all the florists in the vicinity sold anemones only in mixed bunches. Blue? Just blue? What a peculiar idea.

The color of a vase should be dictated by the bouquet it is to hold. Here we decided deliberately to go for a bold approach, playing on the contrast between the cerulean blue of a Wedgwood cache-pot and the muted mauve of several bunches of "Mona Lisa" anemones (left and opposite).

At our fourth vain attempt our minds were made up: we were going to open a shop where people could buy flowers tailored to suit their own particular tastes, moods, and passions.

PRACTICAL GUIDE

1 Here, we use mauve "Mona Lisa" anemones. "Mona Lisa" blooms are larger than those of other anemones, and their centers are more strongly contrasted. The whites are the epitome of elegance, and with their greenish stamens are as graceful as the loveliest hellebores. The blues cover a delicious infinity of shades, from palest violet to deepest purple. The haughty reds are positively regal in their splendor. And the pinks, with their fathomless depths of silky fuchsia, are quite simply sublime…

2 Anemones open quickly in a warm atmosphere and their colors fade with time. It is best to buy them almost in bud, and preferably the day before you want them to look their best.

3 The blooms make a vivid contrast with the cerulean blue of a Wedgwood *cache-pot*, into which crumpled chicken wire has been placed to act as a support to the flowers.

4 Shorten the stems so that only the flowers peep over the brim. Then simply push the stems into the chicken wire.

The perfume-makers's rose

*"Tango" roses are quite
exceptional. Although some
hothouse roses sold by
florists at this time of year
may last longer in water,*

*none can rival the rich
perfume of "Tango." Add
to this their natural grace,
and it is hard to believe that
they are not fresh from the
garden—and that we are in
the depths of winter.*

The rose named "Tango" is cultivated exclusively in the region of Grasse, in Provence, for the use of French perfume-makers. Although it is cultivated under glass—and in stark contrast to other roses at this season, which are invariably unperfumed and rather stiff—"Tango" contrives to offer both the charm and the fragrance of a true garden rose. The dedication of certain rose-growers, who have succeeded in producing this rose for florists, has ensured that "Tango" now takes pride of place among our winter flowers. Buds of modest size unfold to reveal clearly defined blooms in the delicate dusty apricot of *toile de Jouy* and old crushed velvet. Personally, we love them best just as the buds are unfolding, when their coloring is at its subtlest. The petals lighten in color as they open further, revealing a yellow-tinged center, and losing a little of their mystery.

PRACTICAL GUIDE

1 We are particularly fond of marrying this lovely rose with the foliage of eucalyptus, which growers have recently started to color red. Given our preference for natural colors and materials, we tend to view this sort of process with some skepticism, but even we are forced to admit that some types of foliage respond remarkably well to it.

Eucalyptus, for example, becomes most handsome, and here the fine coppery red of its stems harmonizes perfectly with the subtly nuanced coloring of the roses.
2 We chose a spherical metal Art Deco vase to echo the curves of the bouquet, its rich brown tones highlighting the colors of both the roses and the foliage.
3 First strip the roses of their thorns using a knife blade. Pull off the small lateral branches cluttering the base of the eucalyptus stems.
4 Assemble this bouquet like a posy, turning it as you go (see p. 143), and alternating stems of roses and foliage.
5 The shaggy outlines of this bouquet seem to us to flatter the beauty of the roses most naturally, imitating as they do the shape of a rose bush in bloom. To achieve the same effect, take care when assembling the posy to position the roses at different heights. Remember particularly to create a few surprises by submerging some deep in the foliage, so that the eye then has all the pleasure of "discovering" them. Do not on any account attempt to impose a neatly symmetrical shape on this bouquet, or you will destroy all its wayward poetry.
6 Bind the finished bouquet with twine, and trim the stems to fit the vase.

White, mauve, and silver

Not so long ago, silver and silver-gilt vases were so popular that they tended to be used universally, without any attempt to match them with the color of the flowers they were to hold. Metal is a cold material. Blue is a cold color. But mysteriously, in contact with blue flowers, silver glows with a new warmth—and far more so than when partnered with "hot" colors such as red. What is more, polished silver—unlike metals with a patina—invests the blues and mauves of winter with a splendor which is all the more valuable for being unexpected. The reflections mirrored in silver containers are an integral part of their effect, to be anticipated as a feature of the composition. While blues, mauves, and whites produce reflections of glittering purity, yellows produce an unfortunate tarnished effect.

For this composition based on silver vases and goblets, bouquets of a single species cluster round two mixed posies of flowers, berries, and silvery foliage (see following pages).

MUTED ELEGANCE

In the large bucket, the mauve tassels of veronica mingle with the blue-black sheen of *Viburnum tinus* berries among the grey inflorescences of kochia, chosen for their sculptural looks and supple habit. The white ranunculus, meanwhile,

make pools of soft pearly white. This posy was worked loosely and in masses (see p. 143), grouping together each species in small bunches.

SILVER AND BLUE

At its feet, its smaller cousin combines thistle flowers, *Viburnum tinus* berries, and blue grape hyacinths, with the little dove-grey balls of silverbrunia, exotic and long-lasting, adding a festive touch.

ANEMONES

Then come the anemones: anemones, always and for ever. Alone in their splayed vase, they steal the limelight with effortless grace, their deep mauves paling under the influence of the silver. Thanks to their cultivation under glass, we have the luxury of enjoying one of the most exquisite of spring flowers in the depths of winter.

NOSEGAYS

In goblets and a flower-holder, a cluster of nosegays echoes the colors of the larger bouquets, with veronicas, tiny posies of violets, ranunculus, thistles, and a solitary anemone weaving a delicate web of white and mauve, reflected in the gleaming silver of the vases.

Devoted as we are to distressed surfaces and the patinas of age, we remain fascinated by the subtle plays of light and reflections mirrored in gleaming silver vessels.

Seeking the maximum effect, we massed together all our silver containers—buckets, vases, goblets, and a flower-holder—and filled them with a profusion of mauve and white flowers, in loose bouquets and nosegays, tight little posies, and solitary splendor. The rippling reflections of anemones, veronica spikes, ranunculus, and violets seem to intensify the colors of the flowers, while at the same time increasing the luster of the silver.

Posies for flower-trimmed vases

Lacy dried hydrangeas can be used to make "ruffs" to trim wire-covered vases and create a framework for classic winter posies. Here, their muted pastel shades and filigree texture emphasize the dewy freshness and voluptuous smoothness

of creamy "Green" roses and white alstroemeria (above, right, and opposite)

Sometimes it is a pity to spurn a pretty vase in winter simply because its decoration—perhaps of straw or metal wire—seems to make it more appropriate for spring or summer arrangements. Dried hydrangea flowers offer a charming and extremely dainty way of adapting the looks of such vases to winter's needs. It was by accident one day that we stumbled upon this childishly simple way of transforming vases, which has proved a great success among our friends and clients ever since.

PRACTICAL GUIDE

1 We particularly love mixing the prettily muted colors of the hydrangeas with creamy or pink-flushed whites. White refreshes the faded tones of the dried petals, and these in return accentuate the voluptuous density of the fresh blooms.

2 The best method of drying hydrangeas is to put them in vases filled with water, and to let them take up the water without adding any more. In this way, they dry naturally and without wilting. They can also be cut straight from the garden in late October or early November.

3 To trim a vase, start by removing the chrysanthemum stems and fixing a staple (or a tiny length of wire bent into a U-shape) to each bloom.

4 Then attach the chrysanthemum blooms one by one to the rim of the vase so as to create a ruff of petals. The

delicate trimming sets off classic posies perfectly.

5 For these two posies, we chose "Green" roses, with their intriguing hints of menthol green, and a large bunch of white alstroemerias, their lilylike blooms daintily flecked with pink. Alstroemerias have invaded florists' shops and wholesalers in recent years, and with good reason. Reasonably priced and with all the simple virtues of a cottage garden flower, they also come in a wide range of colors, from elegant white, through pastel and coral pink, to clear yellows and warm oranges, which carry fall tints into the depths of winter.

6 The posy should give the impression of resting on the hydrangea ruff, so that the two appear to form a single composition. Trim the stems of the roses and alstroemerias to just the right length to achieve this effect.

7 Then make posies, following the advice on page 143.

A forest of flowers

The reds of certain varieties of amaryllis have the fathomless depth of the finest shot satin. Whether cut very short in a spherical bronze

vase (above) or formed into a stately "tree" with other red flowers (opposite), amaryllis blooms need to be displayed en masse to reveal their full splendor.

Some flowers sold in bunches lend themselves to satisfying arrangements combining equal doses of exhilarating creativity and measured classicism. Making these simple floral "trees" in the depths of winter is a witty and pretty way of anticipating the explosion of blossom that nature holds in store for the spring.

PRACTICAL GUIDE

1 Ranunculus, "Mona Lisa" anemones, and amaryllis blooms, in ascending order, are here used to make three statuesque variations on a theme, all in richly seasonal shades of red.
2 These trees are at their most elegant in containers raised on pedestals, and we personally prefer to group them together, as shown here. If this is not possible, a single urn could be flanked by a pair of shallow bowls piled high with dried and winter fruits.
3 Fill the containers with pre-soaked synthetic foam.
4 Choose the numbers of flowers you are to use according to the size of each container. Take care to be sufficiently generous: too few blooms will make a spindly, unbalanced composition.
5 Make the trees as detailed individually below.
6 Surround each tree with a soft cushion of lichen in delicate shades of almond green. This masks the synthetic foam

and slows down the evaporation rate of the water it holds.
7 The urns look best in uncluttered surroundings. Their sober lines are equally imposing on a marble-topped country table or in a modern interior.

RANUNCULUS

1 Pack the ranunculus blooms, still in bud, tightly together to form a dense ball, then bind them firmly with green string.
2 Then cut the stems diagonally, and push them into the foam to a depth of about one inch.

ANEMONES

1 Buy anemones in tightly bound bunches, so that all you need to do is hold the stems firmly and slip the twine down and off. Three or four bunches will be necessary to create the volume necessary to balance the heavy Medici urn.

AMARYLLIS

Amaryllis blooms are usually sold singly, and are available in shades of white, pink, and red, among which our favorite is this handsome maroon veined with black. The long, straight stems are perfect in appearance for this type of arrangement, but their hollow construction makes them more fragile than they appear.
1 To give them additional support, slide a slender cane up their length, then plunge the canes firmly into the foam. The stems should penetrate the foam to a depth of half an inch or so to enable them to take up water.
2 Start in the middle with the tallest flowers, then circle these with slightly shorter ones, continuing in decreasing height to obtain a majestic pyramidal effect to which the stately amaryllis blooms are perfectly suited.

*T*his sculptural composition, ideal for a setting of oriental inspiration or of uncompromising modernity, combines branches of corkscrew willow with suave tuberoses, a flower of Mexican origin which fills the air with its sweet, heavy, jasmine-like perfume. Held aloft on tall stems, tuberose blooms recall in their outlines the great perfumed *tiare* flowers of Polynesia, their fleshy whiteness attractively flushed with green.

PRACTICAL GUIDE

1 The towering effect of these arrangements is increased by choosing vases that are quite short. This striking sense of visual disproportion is possible only because the two vases used here are heavy enough to support the great length of the branches. The pair of identical bronze Japanese vases accentuate a sense of stylized, rather masculine sobriety.

2 To ensure that the tuberoses last well in water, it is essential to plunge their stems into hot water for at least an hour before arranging them. This practice is advisable for all flowers with stems which exude a white milky liquid, as for example the different varieties of euphorbia.

3 Fill the vases with water, carry them to their display position, and create the arrangements *in situ*, as they are so large.

4 Arrange the willow branches first, as symmetrically as possible. Then add the tuberoses one by one.

5 When the tuberoses have faded, they may easily be replaced with lilies or long-stemmed tulips, which will combine with the willow to create a more intimate effect.

6 In confined spaces, this highly prized feature can be so deliriously intoxicating as to prove overwhelming, and for this reason tuberoses should preferably be displayed in large airy rooms or in passageways.

The slender, soaring stems of tuberoses lend themselves to graphic arrangements of considerable elegance. The delirious headiness of their intoxicating perfume is legendary (opposite).

In an alternative arrangement for a contemporary interior, orchids are placed in little individual tubes (available from garden centers) and arranged among green foliage in a low dish filled with compost and bordered with lichen (above).

Scarlet
and orange

Where flowers are concerned, certain color combinations—blue and yellow, for instance, or purple and pink, seem to form quite spontaneously. We pride ourselves, however, on having "discovered" more unconventional and distinctive color associations, on having brought them into favor, and on having successfully deployed them to woo a faithful clientele who would come to us precisely in order to be amazed. Among these unexpected partnerships, we love the deep mauve of certain anemones beside the tender blue of grape hyacinths, for instance, or bouquets of roses in shades of darkest red and faded lilac. Orange and scarlet together spark off a dialogue of reckless audacity. So reckless, indeed, that one day, at the sight of an arrangement similar to the one shown here, a lady bus conductor drew her bus full of passengers to a screeching halt outside the shop, rushed in to reserve the bouquet, and rushed out again. That evening after work she returned, explaining that she had found the combination of orange ranunculus and red roses so overwhelmingly irresistible that she simply had to have it.

PRACTICAL GUIDE

I In this arrangement, orange ranunculus partner voluptuous "Madame Delbard" roses, the red petals holding deep black shadows with all the depth and sensuality of the subtlest velvet. The orange lends zest to the red and sets up a reciprocal relationship of rich and continuing intensity between the two colors. The mauve of the anemones, meanwhile, acts as a discreet catalyst, shimmering with a curious violet glow beside the blood-red roses. The lavender-blue statice serves as a digression and adds a salutary touch of lightness to this dense bouquet.

2 The curvaceous shape of the capacious bronze vase echoes the voluptuous curves of the flowers. Its somber density, meanwhile, accentuates the dark shadows of the roses, making the air dance with their redness and flash like fire with the orange of the ranunculus.

3 Compose this bouquet of massed flowers (see p. 143), like most of our posies, on the arm: arrange the flowers in bunches against the extended left forearm (for a right-handed person), taking great care never to put two bunches of the same color next to each other while ensuring a harmonious balance of color overall.

4 To create a romantic misty halo of statice above the bouquet, arrange the sprigs so that they stand proud of the other flowers in the posy.

With its reckless combination of orange ranunculus, deepest red roses, purple anemones, and lavender-blue statice, this posy of massed flowers is a virtuoso performance in a range of saturated tones not usually found together. The intensity of its palette harmonizes with the surroundings, and echoes the deep red velvet of the sofa (above and opposite).

Flowers for the office

What sort of flowers are appropriate for an office? Often the decor and furniture are modern, while some of the accessories are almost futuristic, calling for strong compositions with well-defined, forceful lines. Flowers and foliage should observe a certain visual restraint as well as displaying a minimum of backbone. Delicate or voluptuous flowers such as roses or peonies always look out of place in a working atmosphere.

STYLISH FEMININITY

A composition designed for a stylish, rather feminine office features "Apricot Parrot" tulips and two varieties of foliage— eucalyptus and red-flushed leucodendron.

PRACTICAL GUIDE

1 The tulips are luminously beautiful, with petals in sumptuous shades of peach. The berried eucalyptus balances the strong colors of the other two plants, without distracting from the mass of flowers. This foliage is more fruit than leaf, and has a discreet yet powerful presence. The blushing foliage of the leucodendron highlights both the orange of the tulips and the glossy green of the eucalyptus berries.
The contrasting structure of these plants suggests that a triangular-shaped arrangement would work best.
2 Flowers intended for a workplace should always be placed in a heavy, stable vase in order to prevent them from tipping over at the slightest knock. We chose a straight-sided glazed vase to create a fairly dense arrangement.

3 Strip the tulips of most of their leaves so that they take up less space in the vase. Then place them in the foreground in order to draw attention to their petals.
4 Next position the eucalyptus behind and to the left of the tulips. Tease out the branches slightly so that the point of the triangle lies at the same height as the lowest tulip, thus lending volume to the composition as well as an undeniable modernity of spirit.
5 Last, add the leucodendron in a dense mass to contrast with the delicacy of both the tulips and the eucalyptus.

SLEEK MODERNITY

The sober black decor of an emphatically masculine office in Paris, by contrast, inspired an arrangement of exotic flowers.

PRACTICAL GUIDE

1 In a bronze Chinese vase, three spikes of ginger flowers glow amber beside the yellow-green annulated inflorescences of *Calathea lutea*, with the "rattlesnake" calathea ensuring a discreet transition between these two extrovert blooms. A crown of exotic cordyline leaves gives depth to the arrangement.
2 We chose a robust bronze, Chinese vase to emphasize the exotic nature of the plants.
3 Position each species in turn, starting with the most imposing (the ginger spikes), then add the cordyline leaves.

Becoming increasingly popular, exotic flowers are particularly appropriate in a masculine atmosphere (above).

In more feminine surroundings, a massed bouquet of parrot tulips and foliage strikes a note of stylish elegance (opposite).

Homage to the glorious lily

Is it a flower or an insect, this cosseted star-shaped creature turning to face the sun? One of the joys of our profession is the opportunity to make glamorous blooms such as this more widely known (below).

Lilium gloriosa is exoticism incarnate. The mere sight of it is enough to transport susceptible spirits to distant climes, pulsating with tropical heat and color (opposite).

One of the wonderful perks of the florist's trade is the opportunity to make certain rare flowers better known and loved. In this respect, the aptly named *Lilium gloriosa* merits a special place in this book.

This liana of tropical climes is found growing in its natural state in central and southern Africa, and under glass in the Netherlands. On its irregular appearances in other European countries, it is pampered to a degree calculated to make other imported blooms expire in transports of jealousy. Each bloom, shaped like an exquisitely exotic starfish, travels in its own hermetically sealed, air-filled bag, to arrive fresh and sleek, its red and yellow petals having lost none of their glamorous intensity. *Lilium gloriosa*, with its oriental allure straight out of the *Thousand and One Nights*, looks languorously at ease in this crowded Pierre Loti-inspired interior.

PRACTICAL GUIDE

1 With its infinitely lithe and supple stem, its swept-back petals, and its pointed stamens like tiny tongues, *Lilium gloriosa* seems continually in movement, even when perfectly still. It has virtually no foliage, only prehensile leaves constantly in quest of a support around which to twine.

The lilies are partnered with a cloud of *Asparagus miriogladus* foliage, which rises to the occasion with an appropriately exotic air. It would be inappropriate to associate these thrilling and spectacular blooms with more mundane foliage such as laurel or ivy, beside which they would lose some of their glamor and look merely incongruous. Rare blooms require correspondingly rare (or rare-looking) foliage. Otherwise it is preferable to display them on their own, like collector's items.

2 A vase intended to hold a single bloom would perfectly suit this glorious lily. For this ebullient arrangement, however, we chose a glittering red vase to pick up on the color and glamor of the star attraction.

Triumph
in a red vase

Following an occasion when she was presented with a bouquet of carnations after the dress rehearsal of a play, only to be booed on the opening night, Sarah Bernhardt decreed that carnations and pinks bring bad luck. Sadly, succeeding

generations in the superstitious world of the theater have since shunned the unfortunate and blameless flower. This is not enough to deter us, however, from using it to flamboyantly dramatic effect (above and opposite).

There was a time when a red vase had pride of place in our shop. It was a Biot glass vase of a glowing ruby red that we had picked up at an auction and of which we were more than a little proud. Its price was not excessive, and we could never understand why, whenever we proposed it to a client, we were met with a polite but firm refusal, as the client's choice fell invariably on another, and in our view much more ordinary, vase. One day, a kind friend enlightened us: "A red vase? Don't you see? What color flowers can you put in a red vase?"

This bouquet of pinks was the consequence, a spontaneous reaction born of a desire to convince our clients. That week, the Biot vase stood as a beacon in the window, where it did not remain for long before being carried off by a client with the zeal of the converted. Since that time, whenever we sell a red vase or a red bouquet, we are reminded that, in this field as in many others, if you want to communicate your tastes and share the pleasures of your profession, you have to *show* people. True, white flowers and the entire spectrum of yellows and oranges would not do in a red vase, although some blues take on a new and special *éclat*. But for us, a red vase calls above all for a bouquet in all the most outrageous shades of red.

PRACTICAL GUIDE

1 We chose three bunches of pinks, one a hot pinky-red, one veering toward fuchsia, and the last an uncompromising scarlet.

With their spicy fragrance, their sumptuous range of colors, and their long life as cut flowers, pinks deserve to be more popular than they are in France, where they have been rather snubbed over the past twenty years or so. The English are more faithful to them, and it was a visit to the vast greenhouses in which they are cultivated on Guernsey that sealed a close and unbreakable bond between us and pinks.

2 The stems of pinks and carnations are so brittle that it used to be common practice to strengthen them with wire. Newer varieties are less friable, but still need to be handled with care. Keep the stems relatively short so that you can make the most of their suppleness while avoiding the problem of them breaking too easily.

3 Position the bunches of pinks separately in the vase for a bold, massed effect. For a softer arrangement, mix the three bunches, positioning each flower individually.

4 Displayed in this vase that Matisse might have painted, what flower could look more delightful in a contemporary interior? Even the most glacial atmosphere could not remain unmoved by its electrifying, uncompromising redness.

Chrome yellow

*I*nteriors in a contemporary style call for arrangements with clear, unfussy lines and strong colors. When a collector asked us to design a composition for this 1940s smoked glass vase, we decided to fill it with the clear, pure yellow of amaryllis and scented mimosa

in a spontaneous and unpremeditated bouquet.

In their more familiar shades of deep red and snowy white, the showy blooms of amaryllis (more correctly known as hippeastrum) are highly prized during the Christmas season. In order to produce them in this dazzling yellow, growers dose their water with a special dye.

PRACTICAL GUIDE

1 Whatever the color of the flowers, we generally like to soften the stiffness of the hollow stems by associating them with feathery foliage. In this case, the mimosa contributes not only the airy grace of its habit but also the irresistible charm and evocative perfume of its tufted flowerheads. The perfect harmony of colors within this arrangement is stressed and counterpointed by an exhilarating contrast of textures, the pearly smoothness of the amaryllis petals finding their ideal complement in the mimosa's fluffy little balls of golden pollen.

2 Mimosa benefits from a little encouragement to help it last longer in water. Instead of unwrapping bunches of mimosa straight away, trim the ends of the stems, plunge them into scalding water, and leave them for an hour or so before arranging them. This helps to prevent any blockages forming in the ducts through which the stems take up water.

3 The spectacular looks of amaryllis blooms are improved if you remove the withered brown sepals which served originally to protect the unopened buds. It is also a good idea to pierce the hollow stems with a pin just below the flowers: this helps to avoid air pockets forming, which might otherwise prevent water from reaching the flowers.

4 Position the boughs of mimosa first, then simply add the amaryllis.

5 This scented bouquet should last for a good week.

Not a freak of nature but a tribute to the ingenuity of certain growers, pure yellow amaryllis are produced by dosing their water with a special dye. The heady-scented mimosa partners amaryllis in this arrangement. The splendid clarity of the amaryllis is

improved by removing the brown sepals, while mimosa stems are plunged into scalding water. Together they form a composition in startling yellow that is statuesque and highly contemporary (above, left, and opposite).

Sugar and spice

As winter sets in and Christmas draws nearer, the warm, enticing scents of cinnamon sticks, star anise, and cloves capture the lure of distant and exotic lands (below and right).

For this aromatic pot-pourri, destined to scent the air and cheer the spirits throughout the winter months, we have chosen on this occasion a square trough, although a Medici urn would produce an equally sumptuous effect (opposite).

In the winter months, when the house is huddled tight shut, nothing is more evocative than the warm, comforting scents of tropical climes and distant places. This bouquet of spices, like a gift from the Three Kings, is not only deliciously aromatic but also cheeringly spectacular to look at. It is also intriguing to make, whether as a solo effort or a group activity.

PRACTICAL GUIDE

1 For the construction of this aromatic pot-pourri, you need a ball of synthetic foam, a reel of fine brass wire, and a dozen small canes. For the fruits and spices, a selection of clementines (not too ripe in case their skins burst) and pine cones, chestnuts and cinnamon sticks, star anise and cloves fit the bill perfectly.

2 Choose a container that will hold the sphere snugly, while allowing at least two-thirds of the sphere to sit above the rim. We chose a heavy-looking square trough with uncluttered lines which highlights the contrasting textures of the fruit and spices.

3 Place the synthetic foam ball in the container.

4 Stud half the clementines with cloves and the other half with star anise, taking care to let the fruit's lovely orange color show through. Then circle each clementine with wire, twist the wire, and poke the ends into the fruit.

5 Cut the cinnamon sticks into shorter lengths and tie them into small bundles with the wire. Twist the ends of the wire carefully to form a point.

6 Then tie some wire round the bottom of each pine cone and twist it in the same way.

7 Spear the chestnuts and clementines with the sharpened canes, being careful not push the points right through and out the other side.

8 Now the fun can begin. Push the clementines into the foam first, followed by the chestnuts, preferably in clusters. Then fill the gaps with the pine cones and cinnamon sticks, securing them to the foam by their twisted wire tails, adding a final sprinkling of star anise in the same way.

9 An exotic still life such as this is best enjoyed in the cosy atmosphere of a warm, snug living room. Placed near a source of heat, this arrangement will scent the air with its delicious mixture of anise, cinnamon, and cloves—seductive without being overwhelming—throughout the winter months.

Christmas wreaths

*I*In ancient pagan religions, the circle was symbolic of the triumph of life over death. Wreaths of foliage, flowers, or fruit, traditionally made to greet the winter solstice, are now used to decorate many front doors as part of the Christmas festivities.

None of the fir wreaths generally found in the shops at this season can equal the charm of a home-made confection. And making a wreath is not terribly complicated, moreover: provided two or three basic rules of color and balance are observed, it is something anyone can do. For the wreaths we make, we almost always start with a ready-prepared straw frame which we then decorate according to our fancy or the desires of our clients. If the finished wreath is to be hung on a hook or nail, remember to attach a loop to the framework at this stage. Once the wreath is finished, this can easily be disguised with a knot of satin or velvet ribbon or a sprig of foliage.

FROSTED HYDRANGEA WREATH
This ravishingly pretty wreath would look perfect in a romantic bedroom or country sitting room. Hang it close to a source of light to reveal all the subtle play of its delicate shot-silk tones.

PRACTICAL GUIDE
1 Start by cutting off the hydrangea stems just below the flowers.
2 Pin the flowers densely all over the top and sides of the wreath, using hairpins or bent wire.
3 When they are all in place, spray them lightly with aerosol snow or silver paint.
4 Finally, add twenty or so sticks of candied or barley sugar, spearing them into the straw.

In a workshop housed in an old stable adjoining our house, three wreaths wait to find their place among the Christmas decorations. Composed of aromatic foliage (top), lichen and variegated holly (bottom), or simply dried hydrangea flowers (center), they demand a minimum of patience for a maximum of effect.

LICHEN AND VARIEGATED HOLLY WREATH

Lichen is a delightful material to work with, especially when fresh. It is also very evocative, its soft, mossy cushions suggesting silver birch forests and wintry northern landscapes.

PRACTICAL GUIDE

1 If the lichen has dried out, spray it with water and an hour later it will be beautifully soft again.

2 Attach little bouquets of lichen to the straw base with hairpins or bent wire, green for preference, taking care to cover the top and sides, but not the underneath. To create an even effect, bunch the lichen tightly together and flatten it as much as possible as you pin it.

3 All that then remains is to snip branches of variegated holly into pairs of leaves and poke them into the lichen, where they look for all the world like prickly butterflies on a mossy bank.

4 We love the pure simplicity and restrained palette of this wreath exactly

as it is, but it would be equally possible to add holly berries, nuts, or pine cones.

5 This wreath can be made a few days in advance, especially if the lichen is damp when it is bought.

AROMATIC WREATH

This delightfully fragrant wreath is composed of a mixture of four varieties of foliage: thuja, fir, box, and myrtle. Eucalyptus is also marvellous for wreaths, especially as it is available in so many varieties. Used with ivy, it makes fragrant and beautifully fluid arrangements.

PRACTICAL GUIDE

1 Cut all the sprigs to the same length, then use them to make small bunches mixing each of the four varieties.

2 Attach the bunches one by one to the straw base by wrapping a length of very fine wire, preferably green, twice round the stems and the straw. When you have tied on the first one, move on to the second one without cutting the wire.

3 In order to achieve as much fullness as possible, work backward so that each fresh bunch hides the point at which the last one was tied on. Work as evenly and densely as possible over the whole top and sides in order to keep a sense of balance.

4 Aerosol snow or silver paint is decorative when used on fir wreaths. Spray it on unevenly for a more natural effect.

The range of materials that can be used to make wreaths is limited only by the scope of the imagination. For wreaths of different kinds of foliage, tie each little bunch securely to the straw base (left). Pin dried hydrangea flowers individually to the

straw, lightly frost them with an aerosol spray, then add sugar sticks (above).

Red and green Christmas

Ranunculus flowers, asparagus foliage, pyracantha berries, and Viburnum tinus flowers are arranged in a synthetic foam wreath with total freedom, thus

adding a generous dash of imaginative flair. This stage is carried out away from the table, so as to avoid staining the cloth.

When it comes to Christmas decorations, no color scheme appeals to children's imaginations better than red and green. Bright and colorful, it seems to encapsulate the joy written all over their faces in the soft, flickering light of the Christmas candles. Now more than ever, at this magical season when all our dreams seem possible, we love to transform familiar interiors and turn old habits upside down.

Tradition does not have to be dull and dreary. On the contrary, it can be a wonderful source of inspiration which, mixed with lavish doses of aesthetic richness, diversity, and general extravagance, will lend an air of true sumptuousness to the festivities.

TABLE DECORATION

This table decoration consists of a wreath base of synthetic foam decorated with fresh flowers, foliage, and berries.

PRACTICAL GUIDE

1 We chose the almost spherical scarlet ranunculus, the feathery foliage of *Asparagus miriogladus*, holly, and bright red pyracantha berries. Use ranunculus blooms that are as round as possible, but not so large as to be distracting. The grassy asparagus fern contrasts prettily with the shadowy deep green of the holly, and the reds and greens are relieved by the delicate pink-flushed florets of *Viburnum tinus*.

2 Pre-soak the synthetic foam, and place it in the display container.

3 Do not be afraid to exercise complete freedom in arranging the elements of this wreath: it will emphasize the contrasts of textures and add just the right touch of imaginative flair. Start with the foliage, as usual, as it is this that gives the composition its fullness. Gather slender sprays of asparagus into small bunches and poke them into the foam. Then push in individual holly leaves.

4 When this leafy base is finished, prepare the flowers and berries. Trim the stems diagonally, one inch below the flowers, so that they can be arranged with ease and can take up water once in position. Place these, then arrange the viburnum flowers and the pyracantha berries alternately.

5 Place candles in red and green glasses in the center of the decoration; light these before the start of the meal to make the red berries and the satiny ranunculus petals glow.

6 For an oval table, three round table decorations are preferable to a single oval-shaped one, as these tend to be too classic and dull. Three small vases of the same size, or perhaps a central wreath flanked by two smaller ones would create a more charming effect. For a rectangular table, a floral "ribbon" in red and green, a variation on our decoration for a marriage table (see p. 39), would be very suitable.

CHRISTMAS BOUQUET

At once sculptural and voluptuous, this bunched bouquet arranged in a Chambord urn—the shallower cousin of the Medici variety—echoes the colors of the table decoration. In a decorative scheme of this nature it is essential to exploit the colors to the full, finding more or less subtle and ingenious ways of picking up the reds and greens of the table decoration throughout the room. With its imposing shape and size, a bouquet such as this fulfils this role in impressive fashion.

PRACTICAL GUIDE

1 The sumptuous velvety vermilion of "Extase" roses here gains in intensity beside the different greens of two types of exotic "safari plant" foliage—the flat crowns of "Albi Flora" and "Comosum" with its round cones. The different members of this species, widely imported from South Africa at this time of year, imitate the looks of traditional European conifers such as spruce, maritime pine, and larch to perfection. Although rather expensive, they have the advantage of being both very tough and extremely long-lasting in water. Traditional Christmas species such as fir could be used in place of the exotic foliage. What matters most is that any foliage used should have a strong sculptural quality in order to preserve the highly structured appearance of the bouquet.

2 Pre-soak the synthetic foam, and place it in the display container. Lay a protective plastic sheet over the table on which the container is to be displayed.

3 Strip roses of their thorns, and cut the stems of all the plants short to exaggerate the effect of voluptuous, all-enveloping denseness.

4 Anchor massed groups of between seven and ten stems of the same species (see p. 143) in the foam, alternating concentrations of roses with the foliage.

5 As a finishing touch "underplant" the bouquet with billowing cushions of lichen; this is moist and may drip on to the table—hence the protective plastic sheet. For extra flourish, stud this undergrowth with pot hyacinths, masking the pots with fronds of mahonia, the tawny brown undertones of which would echo perfectly the colors of the urn.

Echoing the reds and greens of the table decoration, this sumptuous bouquet mixes the rich vermilion of "Extase" roses with two different types of exotic foliage. The same color theme reverberates around the room, repeated in candles, baubles, and other decorations.

White Christmas

For the table decoration, anchor fragile pure white anemones individually in cubes of synthetic foam (right).

I If children revel in brilliant colors at Chrismas, this is the time of year when adults often crave something simple and stylish, bathed in silvery light and glowing with its own subtle splendor. This, then, is for them: the pure elegance and shimmering reflections of a white Christmas. With corresponding grandeur, the table will be set with fine porcelain, glass, and silver to reflect this world of frosted whiteness.

The steps leading up to the dining room are festooned with a leafy garland, framing the doorway like stage curtains, and opening on to the white table set with sparkling silver and crystal (opposite). Threaded on to the hem with fine gold thread or wire, ivy leaves make a delicately festive edging to the Christmas tablecloth (left).

IVY-LEAF TABLECLOTH DECORATION

A fringe of large ivy leaves hung around the hem will transform a simple white cloth into a model of chic elegance.

PRACTICAL GUIDE

1 Remove the petiole of each leaf, then thread the leaf with fine gold wire or thread.
2 Twist the wire or thread, and pass it through the cloth.
3 For the most stylish effect, leave the wire or thread long enough so that the leaves hang freely.

LEAFY GARLAND

Garlands are among the most traditional and festive of all Christmas decorations, and feasts and celebrations in general have always proved a delightful excuse for decking everything in sight with festoons of flowers and greenery. Inside the house, garlands have a magical ability to transform any corner or recess into a charming retreat. Versatile as well as pretty, they may be caught up in swags to wreathe a mantelpiece, twined luxuriantly up banister rails, festooned in miniature across the frames of pictures and mirrors, or even draped over a hall table or stand.

The foliage of ivy, cedar, fir, and box wreathes the banister rail in a luxuriant garland of greenery (below).

The flickering light of the candles glitters on the artificial snow, the silver, and the crystal glasses, and glows through the translucent veined petals of the anemones. Dreamlike and insubstantial, as though not quite of the real world, this icy, frost-bound landscape has a timeless grace. Simple to assemble, it makes a spectacular centerpiece for a Christmas or New Year's table (opposite).

Although garlands may be bought ready-made, nothing can equal the unique grace and charm of a home-made version. And with a little patience and nimble fingers, anyone can make them.

PRACTICAL GUIDE

1 Here, four types of winter foliage are used: fir, ivy, box, and cedar. Another equally decorative version uses eucalyptus (in flower if possible), asparagus, mahonia, and box. The asparagus foliage will last longer if you spray it with aerosol frost or, if you want to keep it green, aerosol lacquer. Otherwise, the technique is the same.
2 Have ready some green galvanized wire (cloth-covered brass wire is available from garden centers and some florists) and a rope to serve as the backbone: the longer the rope, the longer the finished garland will be.
3 Start by stretching the rope between two hooks or other fixed points about eighteen inches above floor level.
4 Cut up the foliage carefully and make little bunches combining the four species. The longer the stems of the bunches, the more luxuriantly thick the garland will be.
5 Attach the bunches one by one to the rope by winding the brass wire round their stems (without cutting it) in a spiral movement. Position each new bunch so that its leaves hide the stems of the previous one.
6 After the last bunch, wind the brass wire tightly round the garland and cut it. Now you can unhook the ends of the finished garland.

TABLE DECORATION

To show that whiteness is not necessarily synonymous with austerity, we devised this artificial snow decoration to be sprinkled straight on to the tablecloth. Emerging from it, like edelweiss on a snowy mountain top, are white anemones, filmier than the Christmas roses they so closely resemble. The flickering flames of ivory candles in transparent glass holders add pools of warmth in this frozen landscape, glittering on the crystal glasses and revealing the veined translucency of the anemone petals.

PRACTICAL GUIDE

1 For this decoration, the anemones should be fully open so that they look like jewels. To help them unfold, simply put them in a vase close to a source of light or heat.
2 Cut cubes of synthetic foam about one inch across. Soak all the cubes.
3 Then anchor each anemone in a cube of synthetic foam.
4 Arrange the anemones on the table, each on a little square of aluminium foil, and simply scatter the artificial snow between and around them to create as natural an effect as possible. Artificial snow can be bought from florists and some department stores, and is child's play to use. If artificial snow proves difficult to obtain, coarse sea salt can be used to create a very similar effect.
5 Last of all position the candles in their holders on the artificial snow.
6 In fall, a similar sort of decoration could be created using dead leaves, prickly chestnut cases, toadstools, lichen, and so forth.

Basic techniques

Preparing the flowers

Trim the stems of all flowers, whether bought from a florist or picked from the garden, cutting them on the diagonal. This helps them to take up water. Take care also to remove all leaves and flowers that will be below the water level: these might otherwise rot and cause bacteria to form. With a sharp blade remove rose thorns. This not only helps the flowers to take up water but also makes them easier to handle,

especially if they are to be mixed with other species in a more elaborate composition.

Crush the ends of the woody branches of spring-flowering shrubs and trees, such as lilac and cherry, with a hammer. This prevents scars

from sealing off vessels in the wood which carry water to the flowers. Many summer species such as willows and dogwood benefit from the same treatment. An equally effective alternative is to cut a cross into the length of the stem to a depth

of an inch or two.

Flowers such as daffodils and euphorbias secrete a sap from their stems which can be harmful to other flowers. Plunge them in a bucket of hot water for a couple of hours before arranging them.

Supporting the flowers

Only narrow-necked vases provide sufficient support for flowers on their own. In wide-necked containers, use a traditional flower-holder or crumpled chicken wire, which is easy to mold to the required shape. Glass vases need flower-holders that are both effective and aesthetic. No flower-arranger would willingly be without stones, pebbles, and coarse sand—all easy to use and attractive to look at.

A neat trick for providing support is to stick a grid of adhesive tape over the neck of the vase, a highly effective method of holding the flowers which

becomes progressively invisible as the flowers are added.

Synthetic or florist's foam is also very convenient. Cut it to fit inside the base of the container, and saturate it in boiling water (without submerging it). Then place it in the container—it can be used in any non-transparent container and is particularly useful for heavy autumn containers and for putting the finishing touches to Christmas decorations. It is a reliable way of transforming all sorts of vessels into watertight vases. It is not reusable. Synthetic mousse adapts itself instantly to any requirements, whether placed on a shallow dish or on a sheet of cellophane at the bottom of a metal or straw basket, or tucked into a cracked jug or porous cachepot. Anchoring flowers in it is child's play, but once you have made your arrangement, remember to top up the water as necessary.

Choosing the vase

Containers in any shape and material may be suitable for holding a branch, a single flower, or a mixed bouquet. Materials tend to vary with the season. Glass is wonderful for playing with light effects in spring, but in fall it gives way to heavier materials, especially metal, more appropriate to the earthy colors of

October arrangements. Similarly, while the profuse bouquets of summer sit happily in brightly glazed earthenware pots or sky-blue enamel jugs, the rarer blooms of winter need to be flattered with porcelain cups, silver goblets, or engraved glass. Vases may be tall or squat, straight-sided or splayed, spherical or wide-necked, irrespective of season. Tall, oval-shaped vases are best for freely mixed bouquets or arrangements including tall spikes such as

delphiniums or lupins, while posies are at home in almost anything. The vase should reflect the shape of the bouquet, complementing and balancing it. Thus the same vase, used to hold either an arrangement of spreading branches or a tight posy that perches on top of it like a lid (see p.140), may take on two completely different appearances. From old beakers to abandoned garden urns, any container may be turned into a vase. To support the

flowers all you need is an appropriate flower-holder, as described above, and if the neck is narrow enough you may not need one at all. Thanks to synthetic mousse, the range of classic vases has been broadened to include almost anything you can think of. Shells, teapots, bowls, baskets in metal or straw, cracked cups—all these and more can now be filled with flowers to cheer the house.

Making a posy

Very much in vogue over the last decade or so, posies are a perfect way of creating direct contrasts of flower color and shape. Their half-spherical shape looks well in most containers, and we like to present them wrapped in colored tissue paper.

Posies are not difficult to make. If you are right-handed, start by grasping a stem between the thumb and index finger of your left hand. Add a second stem, crossing it over the first one so that the flower lies to the left of the original one. Continue in this way with the other stems, crossing them and turning the hand counter-clockwise as you do so. When the posy is finished, bind the stems at the point at which they meet with twine or string, then trim them as necessary. It is very important to remember that the size of the posy is dictated by the point at which the stems cross. The higher the binding point, the tighter the posy; conversely, the lower the binding point, the more voluminous the posy will be.

Making a "bunched" bouquet

Nearly all the bouquets we sell in our shop are massed in bunches of different species or colors. By their nature, these are large bouquets including a number of bunches of flowers or foliage, and playing on their contrasts of color and texture. To make a "bunched" bouquet, first select your flowers and clean the stems, then group them into bunches of several stems of the same type, binding each bunch with twine. The number of stems in a bunch will vary with the size of the flower. On average, you

will need about ten in each bunch of roses, and only two or three of larger blooms such as showy dahlias.

Then arrange the bound bunches on the left forearm (if you are right-handed), playing with the groupings with the right hand until just the right effects of color and texture are achieved, taking care not to juxtapose two identical bunches.

When all the bunches are positioned to your satisfaction, arrange them in a wide-necked vase. These dense bouquets need a lot of water, so remember to top up the level daily.

Acknowledgments

Pierre Brinon and Philippe Landri would like to thank
Monsieur and Madame Jean-Pierre Arbon who first launched this
project, as well as Gisou Bavoillot, Marc Walter,
and the entire editorial team for their support during the creation
of this book. Sincere thanks also go to Mademoiselle
Françoise Fabian, Madame Laurence Drisin (of the Société GALD),
and in particular Monsieur Jean-Louis Scherrer,
who by lending their beautiful possessions, or by welcoming
the authors into their homes have contributed greatly to the success
of this book.

Olivier de Vleeschouwer would like to thank his friends at
Mille Feuilles for giving him the privilege of writing about their
common passion for flowers and gardens.
He also thanks Gisou Bavoillot for her perfectionism,
and Nathalie Bailleux for her editing and helpful advice.

The Publisher extends thanks to the team who worked on this book:
Marc Walter whose design elegantly presents Christophe Dugied's
beautiful photography; Murielle Vaux who took care of the
production, Patrizia Tardito for her careful photoengraving, and also
Nathalie Bailleux, Anne-Laure Mojaïsky, Véronique Manssy,
Soazig Cudennec, and Valérie Vidal.

les mille feuilles
les mille feuilles
les mille feuilles

2 RUE RAMBUTEAU 75003 PARIS
TEL. 01 42 78 32 93